Easy to Read
LARGE PRINT

3-MINUTE devotions FOR WOMEN

180 INSPIRATIONAL READINGS FOR HER HEART

BARBOUR
PUBLISHING

ISBN 979-8-89151-115-6

Text previously published as *Choose Hope: 3-Minute Devotions for Women*.

Cover Design: Greg Jackson, Thinkpen Design

Published by Barbour Publishing, Inc., 1810 Barbour Drive, Uhrichsville, Ohio 44683, www.barbourbooks.com

Our mission is to inspire the world with the life-changing message of the Bible.

Printed in China.

INTRODUCTION

God, the one and only—I'll wait as long as he says. Everything I hope for comes from him, so why not? He's solid rock under my feet, breathing room for my soul. . .I'm set for life.

PSALM 62:5–6 MSG

These devotions are especially for those days when you need a bit of encouragement. Three minutes from your busy day is all you'll need to refresh your spirit and fill your cup to overflowing with hope for the journey.

- Minute 1: Read and reflect on God's Word.
- Minute 2: Read the devotion and think about how it applies to your life.
- Minute 3: Pray.

Although these devotions aren't meant as a tool for deep Bible study, they can be a touchstone to keep you grounded and focused on God, the giver of all good things. May this book remind you that hopeful expectation may be woven into life's everyday moments.

Easy to Read
LARGE PRINT

3-MINUTE devotions FOR WOMEN

EVEN MORE!

Now unto him that is able to do exceeding abundantly above all that we ask or think, according to the power that worketh in us.

EPHESIANS 3:20 KJV

"Above all that we ask or think" is just that. Imagine every good thing that God has promised in His Word—or things you've only dreamed about. Think of wonderful things that exceed the limits of human comprehension or description, then imagine that God is able and *willing* to do even more!

The last part of this verse indicates that the Holy Spirit works within the Christian's life to accomplish the seemingly impossible. Our highest aspirations are within God's power—but like Paul, we must pray. When we do, God does far more for us than we could ever guess.

O Lord, You accomplish things I perceive as impossible. You know my hopes and dreams, and I believe that You are able to exceed my greatest expectations. Amen.

REVEAL THE HOPE

In your hearts revere Christ as Lord. Always be prepared to give an answer to everyone who asks you to give the reason for the hope that you have. But do this with gentleness and respect.

1 PETER 3:15 NIV

Isn't the relevance of God's Word amazing? Peter gives three parts of advice with several key words. First, Peter advises to set God apart from everything else in your heart; in other words, "sanctify" or recognize God's holiness and treat Him with deserved awe. Second, be prepared to explain your hope in Christ and eternal life, having a full grasp of what and in whom you believe. Finally, remember *how* you say something is equally important to *what* you say. In other words, we must walk the walk before we can reveal the hope we have in Jesus Christ.

Dear God, please prepare me to explain my hope in Christ and eternal life. Teach me to explain it in a way that honors You with gentleness and respect. Amen.

STRENGTH IN HOPE

I say to myself, "The Lord is my portion;
therefore I will wait for him."

LAMENTATIONS 3:24 NIV

In this verse, the writer declares that the Lord is his portion. The Lord is our portion too. But when will we fully receive this inheritance and celebrate with Him? We know it is coming, but it's difficult to wait. Hope gives us strength as we anticipate our return to God. We belong to God and know someday we will worship Him face-to-face in His presence. Knowing God will keep His promise, we can say with confidence, "The Lord is my portion; therefore I will wait."

What an amazing promise You have made to me,
Father, that one day I will be with You in heaven.
My hope is in You as I wait for that day. Amen.

PLANTED DEEP

Fix these words of mine in your hearts and minds; tie them as symbols on your hands and bind them on your foreheads.

DEUTERONOMY 11:18 NIV

Memorizing Bible verses isn't a fashionable trend in today's world, but learning key verses plants the Word of God deeply in our hearts. We draw strength and nourishment in dark times from remembering what God told us in the Bible. In times of crisis, we recall God's promises of hope and comfort. In our everyday moments, repeating well-known verses reminds us that God is always with us—whether we feel like it or not.

What an awesome gift You have given me, God—the Bible! I will fix Your words in my mind and heart and carry them with me wherever I go. Amen.

KNOW THE HOPE

I pray that the eyes of your heart may be enlightened in order that you may know the hope to which he has called you, the riches of his glorious inheritance in his holy people, and his incomparably great power for us who believe.

EPHESIANS 1:18–19 NIV

Our heart is central when it comes to God. It's not only vital for our physical life but our spiritual life as well. It's the thinking apparatus of our soul, containing all our thoughts, passions, and desires. Why was Paul so anxious for Christians to make heartfelt spiritual progress? Because of the payoff! God freely offers us His incomparably great power along with a rich, glorious inheritance. We just have to see our need for a little surgery.

Instill in me a new heart, God. Fill it with Your unrivaled power and love. Place within it the priceless gift of Jesus' sacrifice and the promise of eternal life in heaven. Amen.

GOD HEARS

I love the LORD because he hears my voice and my prayer for mercy.

PSALM 116:1 NLT

Psalm 116:1 is a wonderful verse that should not be missed. It is neither lament nor praise, as are many of the other psalms, but it is a strong assurance of hope. Whether we are offering our praise to God or falling at His feet with our struggles, we know from these few words that God hears us. Isn't that mind-blowing? The Almighty God of the universe who created and assembled every particle in existence hears us when we come before Him.

I have so many reasons to love You, Lord, so many reasons to worship and praise You. How grateful I am that You hear my voice! I love You, Lord. Amen.

RENEWED HOPE AND FAITH

I am Alpha and Omega, the beginning and the end, the first and the last.

REVELATION 22:13 KJV

In the Old Testament, the Lord God called Himself a shepherd, the Alpha and Omega, the Beginning and the End, and the Almighty. He is called the First and the Last. In the New Testament, we find the same titles given to Jesus. The Bible is unique because in it God fully reveals who He is. Since Jesus is fully God, let it renew our hope and faith in our Savior. He who created all things out of nothing will re-create this world into a paradise without sin.

Jesus, I learn how to live by Your human example, and I trust in You as my God—Father, Son, and Holy Spirit—three persons, one God, one perfect You! Amen.

HOPE THRIVES

"For I know the plans I have for you," declares the Lord, "plans to prosper you and not to harm you, plans to give you hope and a future."

Jeremiah 29:11 NIV

Hope thrives in the fertile soil of a heart restored by a loving gesture, a compassionate embrace, or an encouraging word. It is one of God's most precious gifts. God *wants* to forgive our sins and lead us on the paths of righteousness—just as He did for the Israelites of old. He has great plans for us. That's His promise, and our blessed hope.

Father, You provide hope when all seems hopeless. Trusting in Your plans for me brings me joy. My future is in Your hands, so how can it be anything but good? Amen.

CONFIDENT HOPE

For you have been my hope, Sovereign Lord, my confidence since my youth.

Psalm 71:5 NIV

Internal clues suggest that the psalmist wrote Psalm 71 during a troublesome time. In the midst of recounting his situation, he asserted that God had been his hope and confidence since his youth. As Paul later outlined in Romans 5, his previous experiences built that hope. Confidence in the Lord allows us to face disasters without fear (Proverbs 3:25–26), to live in peace (Isaiah 32:17), and to approach God (Ephesians 3:12). In an unpredictable world, we serve an unchanging God who has earned our confidence.

Father, in this ever-changing, fast-paced world, I find comfort knowing that You never change. My confidence is in You with a good outcome guaranteed. Amen.

EXPECTANT HOPE

In the morning, Lord, you hear my voice;
in the morning I lay my requests before
you and wait expectantly.

Psalm 5:3 NIV

God fulfills His side of the bargain to hear our prayers. Then we take off on our merry way, trying to solve our dilemma without Him. We leave His presence without lingering with the Lord to listen and to worship Him in the silence of our heart. Then later we return with more demands and *gimmes*. God knows our human hearts and understands. He gently waits to hear from us, and He delights when we keep our end of the bargain and linger in His light with hearts full of anticipation and hope.

Dear God, my hope is in You. Thank You for listening to my prayers and knowing exactly what I need. I wait patiently, expectantly, knowing that You will answer me. Amen.

LOVE SONG OF FORGIVENESS

"In that day," declares the L*ORD*, *"you will call me 'my husband'; you will no longer call me 'my master.'"*

HOSEA 2:16 NIV

God wants *our* hearts. He desires a relationship with us based on love and forgiveness. He enters into a covenant with us like the marriage between Hosea and Gomer. God is the loving, faithful husband, constantly pursuing us no matter what we do or where we roam. Though it is difficult to grasp how much He loves us, we find hope in His promise. God will keep His commitment to us. His love song to us is forgiveness, and His wedding vow is unconditional love.

Thank You for loving me so fully and unconditionally, God. I find comfort knowing that as much as any man on earth could love me, You love me more. Amen.

ONLY BELIEVE

While Jesus was still speaking, some people came from the house of Jairus, the synagogue leader. "Your daughter is dead," they said. "Why bother the teacher anymore?"

MARK 5:35 NIV

When the odds are stacked against us and circumstances riddle us with hopelessness, our tendency is to manage our burdens as well as we can and stop praying. Doubtful, we wonder: *Can God restore an unhappy marriage? Can He heal cancer? Can He deliver me from financial ruin?* Will *He*? Jesus knows the way out. Only believe; have faith in Him and never lose hope.

Jesus, my hope is in You. Even when it appears that all hope is lost, I will hold onto the hope that You will deliver me. Amen.

SEEKING GOD'S PLAN

For we are His workmanship, created in Christ Jesus for good works, which God prepared beforehand that we should walk in them.

EPHESIANS 2:10 NKJV

How can you know God's plans for your life? First, you should meet with Him in prayer each day and seek His will. Studying the Bible is also important. Often, God speaks to us directly through His Word (Psalm 119:105). Finally, you must have faith that God *will* work out His plan for your life and that His plan is good. Jeremiah 29:11 (NIV) says, "'For I know the plans I have for you,' declares the LORD, 'plans to prosper you and not to harm you, plans to give you hope and a future.'" Are you living in Christ's example and seeking God's plan for your life?

Father, what is Your plan for me? I know that it is good. Reveal it to me, Lord. Speak to me through prayer and Your Word. Amen.

GOOD NEWS

These are evil times, so make every minute count.

EPHESIANS 5:16 CEV

While it may seem tempting to crawl back into bed and hide beneath the covers of denial instead of facing the harsh reality of the world, God has a different idea. Every minute counts because we, as believers, carry an eternal hope that the world needs to hear. Bad things do happen to good people, but ever-present in the trials of this world is a loving God who cares deeply for His children. Who will you share this good news with today?

Dear God, how should I share the good news with those who have suffered at the hand of evil? Show me ways to encourage them that You love and care for them. Amen.

BEHIND THE SCENES

Now faith is confidence in what we hope for and assurance about what we do not see.

HEBREWS 11:1 NIV

Be encouraged today that no matter what takes place in the natural—what you see with your eyes—it doesn't have to be the final outcome of your situation. If you've asked God for something, then you can trust that He is working out all the details behind the scenes.

What you see right now, how you feel, is not a picture of what your faith is producing. Your faith is active, and God is busy working to make all things come together and benefit you.

Heavenly Father, what I see today is not what I'm going to get. Thank You for working behind the scenes to bring about the very best for my life. Amen.

RELEASING YOUR HOLD ON ANXIETY

Search me, God, and know my heart; test me and know my anxious thoughts. See if there is any offensive way in me, and lead me in the way everlasting.

Psalm 139:23–24 NIV

What is it that weighs you down? Financial issues? An unhealthy relationship? Your busy schedule? Surrender these misgivings to a God who wants to take them from you. Ask Him to search your heart for any and all anxieties, for any and all signs that you have not truly put your trust in Him. Find the trouble spots in your life to which you direct most of your thoughts and energy, and then hand these troubles over to one who can truly address them.

Realize that you are only human, and that God is infinitely more capable of balancing your cares than you are.

Lord, take from me my anxieties, big and small. May I remember to give these to You daily so that I will not find myself distracted by the things of this world.

POWER-PACKED AND PERSONAL

Thou hast magnified thy word above all thy name.

PSALM 138:2 KJV

Of all the wonderful graces and gifts God has given humankind, there's nothing that touches the power and truth of that all-time bestseller, the Bible. The Bible provides healing, hope, and direction (Psalm 107:20; 119:74, 133). If we want wisdom and the desire to do things the right way, God's Word equips us (2 Timothy 3:16–17). From the scriptures we can make sense of a confusing world. We can get a hold on real truth. God has given us His eternal Word to know Him and to know ourselves better.

Teach me not only to read but also to obey Your living, powerful Word every day, Lord God. Amen.

STANDING STILL

"The Lord will fight for you;
you need only to be still."
Exodus 14:14 NIV

Moses commanded the Israelites to stop panicking and stand still. Then God held back the waters of the Red Sea, and the Israelites were able to walk across on dry ground! When the Egyptians tried to follow them, the waters rushed in and drowned them all.

Sometimes when we stress and panic, we rack our brains trying to figure out solutions to our problems; and instead of standing still and praying to God, we become even more panicked. Moses' words still apply to us today. When we face our fears, we should be still, trusting in God and relying on Him to bring us through the struggle.

Dear Lord, please teach me to be still and to trust in You. Thank You for Your constant faithfulness. Amen.

THE BLUES

Why, my soul, are you downcast? Why so disturbed within me? Put your hope in God, for I will yet praise him, my Savior and my God.

PSALM 42:11 NIV

Everyone experiences times when frustrations seem to outweigh joy, but as Christians, we have an unending source of encouragement in God.

That's great, you may think, *but how am I supposed to tap into that joy?* First, pray. Ask God to unburden your spirit. Share your stress, frustrations, and worries with Him. Don't hold back; He can take it. Make a list of the blessings in your life and thank the provider of those blessings. Choose to not focus on yourself; instead, praise Him for being Him.

Soon you'll feel true, holy refreshment—the freedom God wants you to live out every day.

Rejuvenate my spirit, Lord! You alone can take away the burden I feel. You are my hope and my redeemer forever. Amen.

ROCK SOLID

"Therefore everyone who hears these words of mine and puts them into practice is like a wise man who built his house on the rock. The rain came down, the streams rose, and the winds blew and beat against that house; yet it did not fall, because it had its foundation on the rock."

MATTHEW 7:24–25 NIV

Prepare for tomorrow's storms by laying a solid foundation today. Rain and wind are guaranteed to come. It is only a matter of time. We need to be ready. When our foundation is the Rock, Jesus Christ, we will find ourselves still standing when the storm has passed.

Rain will come. Winds will blow and beat hard against us. Yet, when our hope is in the Lord, we will not be destroyed. We will remain steadfast because our feet have been firmly planted. Stand upon the Rock today so that your tomorrows will be secure.

Dear Lord, help me build my foundation today upon You so I can remain steadfast in the storms of life. Amen.

GOD'S WORK

The Lord will perfect that which concerns me; Your mercy, O Lord, endures forever; do not forsake the works of Your hands.

Psalm 138:8 NKJV

The psalmist offers hope when he tells us the Lord will complete things that concern us. We are the work of His hands, and He has enduring mercy toward our failures. He is as active in our sanctification as He is in our salvation. Philippians 1:6 (NKJV) says, "Being confident of this very thing, that He who has begun a good work in you will complete it until the day of Jesus Christ." The power to change or to see difficult things through to the end comes from the Lord, who promises to complete the work He begins.

Lord, remind me of this word when I am discouraged by my lack of progress. Help me remember Your eternal love and mercy to me. Give me confidence that You will complete me.

HOLDING ON TO HOPE

"In this world you will have trouble.
But take heart! I have overcome the world."
JOHN 16:33 NIV

Christ tells us to hold on to the hope we have in Him. He tells us to *"take heart"* because the trials of this world have already been won, the evil has already been conquered, and He has already overcome the world. Live your life as a statement of hope, not despair. Live like the victor, not the victim. Live with your eye on eternity, not the here and now. Daily remind yourself that you serve a powerful and gracious God, and decide to be used by Him to act as a messenger of grace and healing to the world's brokenness.

Lord, forgive my doubts. Forgive me for growing discouraged and not placing my full trust in You. May I learn to trust You better and to live my life as a statement of hope.

RESCUED

God rescued us from dead-end alleys and dark dungeons. He's set us up in the kingdom of the Son he loves so much, the Son who got us out of the pit we were in, got rid of the sins we were doomed to keep repeating.

COLOSSIANS 1:13–14 MSG

The message of the gospel doesn't leave us trapped in our sin and misery without hope. God sent the rescuer, Christ, who plucked us out of the dungeons of despair and into His kingdom of light and strength to overcome the dragons of sin. It's by the Father's grace that we are not stuck in our habitual ruts and dead-end alleys, living without purpose and fulfillment. We walk in His kingdom—a kingdom that goes counter to the world's ideas. We are out of the pit, striding confidently in Him, enjoying life to its fullest.

Glory to You, Jesus! You have rescued me from the pit and lifted me to Your kingdom of real life and victory. Help me to walk in that fact today. Amen.

JOYFUL, PATIENT, AND FAITHFUL

Be joyful in hope, patient in affliction, faithful in prayer.

ROMANS 12:12 NIV

Faithfulness in prayer requires discipline. God is faithful regardless of our attitude toward Him. He never changes, wavers, or forsakes His own. We may be faithful to do daily tasks around the house. We feed the cat, wash the clothes, and empty the trash. But faithfulness in the quiet discipline of prayer is harder. There are seemingly no consequences for neglecting our time with the Lord. Oh, what a myth this is! Set aside a daily time for prayer, and see how the Lord blesses you, transforming your spirit to increase your joyful hope, your patience, and your faithfulness.

Faithful God, find me faithful. Stir up the hope and joy within me. Give me the grace I need to wait on You. Amen.

UNBROKEN PROMISE

In hope of eternal life which God,
who cannot lie, promised before time began.
TITUS 1:2 NKJV

God always keeps His word. The Bible is filled with the promises of God—vows to us that we can trust will be completed. God never lies. Lying is not in Him. He sees us as worthy of His commitment. The promise of eternal life—given even before time began—is one of God's most wonderful gifts. No matter how disappointed we are with ourselves or with others, we only have to look at the pledge God has made to be filled with a heart of praise and gladness.

God, thank You that Your Word is trustworthy and true. Praise You for the promise of eternal life. Amen.

A MATTER OF PRIORITIES

To everything there is a season,
a time for every purpose under heaven.
ECCLESIASTES 3:1 NKJV

Only one thing in our lives never changes: God. When our world swirls and threatens to shift out of control, we can know that God is never surprised, never caught off guard by anything that happens. Just as He guided David through dark nights and Joseph through his time in prison, God can show us a secure way through any difficulty. He can turn the roughest times to good. Just as He supported His servants in times past, He will always be with us, watching and loving.

Lord, help me remember Your love and guidance when my life turns upside down. Grant me wisdom for the journey and a hope for the future. Amen.

REMEMBER THIS

Keep your eyes on Jesus, who both began and finished this race we're in.

HEBREWS 12:2 MSG

When our heads are spinning and tears are flowing, there is only one thing to remember: focus on Jesus. He will never leave you nor forsake you. When you focus on Him, His presence envelops you. Where there is despair, He imparts hope. Where there is fear, He imparts faith. Where there is worry, He imparts peace. He will lead you on the right path and grant you wisdom for the journey. When the unexpected trials of life come upon you, remember this: focus on Jesus.

Dear Lord, I thank You that nothing takes You by surprise. When I am engulfed in the uncertainties of life, help me remember to focus on You. Amen.

UNSWERVING FAITH

Let us hold unswervingly to the hope we profess, for he who promised is faithful.

HEBREWS 10:23 NIV

The author of Hebrews challenges us to hold *unswervingly* to our hope in Christ Jesus. Certainly we fail to do this at times, but life is much better when we keep our eyes fixed on Him. Sometimes just a whisper from Satan, the father of lies, can cause shakiness where once there was steadfastness. Place your hope in Christ alone. He will help you to resist the lies of this world. Hold *unswervingly* to your Savior today. He is faithful!

Jesus, You are the object of my hope. There are many distractions in my life, but I pray that You will help me to keep my eyes on You. Thank You for Your faithfulness. Amen.

WHAT RICHES DO YOU POSSESS?

Command those who are rich. . .not to be arrogant nor to put their hope in wealth, which is so uncertain, but to put their hope in God, who richly provides us with everything for our enjoyment.

1 TIMOTHY 6:17 NIV

God desires to bless us with possessions we can enjoy. But it displeases Him when His children strain to attain riches in a worldly manner out of pride or a compulsion to flaunt. Riches are uncertain, but faith in God to meet our provisions is indicative of the pure in heart. Pride diminishes the capacity for humility and trust in God. We are rich indeed when our hope and faith are not in what we have but in whom we trust.

Heavenly Father, my hope is in You for my needs and my desires. I surrender any compulsion to attain earthly wealth; rather, may I be rich in godliness and righteousness. Amen.

REALITY CHECK

Instead, you must worship Christ as Lord of your life. And if someone asks about your hope as a believer, always be ready to explain it. But do this in a gentle and respectful way. Keep your conscience clear. Then if people speak against you, they will be ashamed when they see what a good life you live because you belong to Christ.

1 PETER 3:15–16 NLT

Every day we are being watched—both by the Father and by the people around us. Our attitudes and speech often are weighed against beliefs we profess and the hope we claim. Take time to search your heart and your motivations. If your speech and attitude aren't Christ-centered, re-aim your heart to hit the mark.

Lord, help me to be a good representative for You. Amen.

PERSEVERING THROUGH ADVERSITY

"But if it is from God, you will not be able to stop these men; you will only find yourselves fighting against God." His speech persuaded them. They called the apostles in and had them flogged. Then they ordered them not to speak in the name of Jesus, and let them go. The apostles left the Sanhedrin, rejoicing because they had been counted worthy of suffering disgrace for the Name.

ACTS 5:39–41 NIV

Scripture overflows with stories of God's beloved children undergoing extreme hardships. Just because we have faith, hope, and trust in the Lord does not mean that life will be easy. Instead, God's love for us means that He will provide a way *through*, not around, adversity, resulting in His greater glory. Everyone experiences tough times. The goal, however, is not to find relief. It is to live in a way that shows how well we love and trust the Lord.

Father God, I know that no matter how troubled my life is, You can provide me a way to persevere. Help me to trust Your guidance and love. Amen.

DAYBREAK

"As your days, so shall your strength be."
DEUTERONOMY 33:25 NKJV

There are times in life when we feel that the night season we're facing will last forever and a new morning will never come. For those particularly dark seasons of your life, you don't have to look to the east to find the morning star, but instead find that morning star in your heart. Allow the hope of God's goodness and love to rekindle faith. With the passing of the night, gather your strength and courage. A new day is dawning, and with it, new strength for the journey forward. All that God has promised will be fulfilled.

Heavenly Father, help me to hold tightly to faith, knowing in this situation that daybreak is on its way. Amen.

FINDING BALANCE

Hope deferred makes the heart sick,
but when the desire comes, it is a tree of life.
PROVERBS 13:12 NKJV

Jesus is your hope! He stands a short distance away bidding you to take a walk on water—a step of faith toward Him. Let Him direct you over the rough waters of life, overcoming each obstacle one opportunity at a time. Don't look at the big picture in the midst of the storm, but focus on the one thing you can do at the moment to help your immediate situation—one step at a time.

Lord, help me not to concentrate on the distractions, but to keep my focus on which step to take next in order to reach You. Amen.

A FRESH NEW HARVEST

*Do not rejoice over me, my enemy;
when I fall,I will arise; when I sit in darkness,
the LORD will be a light to me.*

MICAH 7:8 NKJV

The enemy of your soul wants you to consider each failure and dwell on the past, fully intending to rob you of your future. But God wants you to take that seed of hope that seems to have died and bury it in His garden of truth—trusting Him for a new harvest of goodness and mercy. Once you have buried that seed deep in the ground of God's love, it will grow and become a part of His destiny for your life.

Lord, help me not to focus on the past but to look to You every step of the way. Amen.

WEARY DAYS

Why art thou cast down, O my soul? and why art thou disquieted in me? hope thou in God: for I shall yet praise him for the help of his countenance. O my God, my soul is cast down within me: therefore will I remember thee from the land of Jordan, and of the Hermonites, from the hill Mizar.

PSALM 42:5–6 KJV

Our willingness to speak with God at the day's beginning shows our dependence on Him. We can't make it alone. It is a comforting truth that God never intended for us to trek through the hours unaccompanied. He promises to be with us. He also promises His guidance and direction as we meet people and receive opportunities to serve Him. Getting started is as simple as removing our head from beneath the pillows and telling God good morning.

Lord, refresh my spirit and give me joy for today's activities. Amen.

RELEASE THE MUSIC WITHIN

Those who are wise will find a time
and a way to do what is right.
ECCLESIASTES 8:5 NLT

It has been said that many people go to their graves with their music still in them. Do you carry a song within your heart, waiting to be heard? Whether we are eight or eighty, it is never too late to surrender our hopes and dreams to God. A wise woman trusts that God will help her find the time and manner in which to use her talents for His glory as she seeks His direction. Let the music begin.

Dear Lord, my music is fading against the constant beat of a busy pace. I surrender my gifts to You and pray for the time and manner in which I can use those gifts to touch my world. Amen.

IT'S ALL GOOD

And we know that all things work together for good to them that love God, to them who are the called according to his purpose.

ROMANS 8:28 KJV

God can and does use all things in our lives for His good purpose. Remember Joseph in the cistern, Daniel in the lions' den, and Jesus on the cross? The Lord demonstrated His resurrection power in each of those cases. He does so in our lives as well. He brings forth beauty from ashes.

What are you facing that seems impossible? What situation appears hopeless? What circumstance is overwhelming you? Believe God's promise.

Dear Lord, thank You that You work all things together for Your good purpose. May I trust You to fulfill Your purpose in my life. Amen.

DARKNESS INTO LIGHT

We can rejoice, too, when we run into problems and trials, for we know that they help us develop endurance. And endurance develops strength of character, and character strengthens our confident hope of salvation.

ROMANS 5:3–4 NLT

Whether it's an illness, job loss, strained friendship, or even the everyday challenges that sneak up, we want to find the quickest way out. Fortunately, we have a loving God who promises to stay beside us through the darkness. Even though night does come, the quickest way to see the morning is to take God's hand and walk through the hard times. In the morning, the sun rises and the darkness fades, but God is still there. God never promised that our lives would be easy, but He did promise that He would always be with us—in the darkness and all through the night.

God, thank You for being a constant source of comfort and dependability in my life. Amen.

JONAH'S PRAYER

"When my life was ebbing away,
I remembered you, LORD, and my prayer
rose to you, to your holy temple."
JONAH 2:7 NIV

In verse 6 of his great prayer from the belly of the fish, we read these words: *"But you, LORD my God, brought my life up from the pit."* When Joseph reached a point of desperation, he realized that God was his only hope. Have you been there? Not in the belly of a great fish, but in a place where you are made keenly aware that it is time to turn back to God? God loves His children and always stands ready to receive us when we need a second chance.

Father, like Jonah I sometimes think my own ways are better than Yours. Help me to be mindful that Your ways are always good and right. Amen.

BE STILL AND LEARN

His delight and desire are in the law of the Lord, and on His law (the precepts, the instructions, the teachings of God) he habitually meditates (ponders and studies) by day and by night.

PSALM 1:2 AMPC

It takes discipline to spend time with the Lord, but that simple discipline helps to keep our hope alive, providing light for our paths. When the schedule seems to loom large or the weariness of everyday living tempts you to neglect prayer and Bible study, remember they are your lifeline. They keep you growing in your relationship with the lover of your soul.

Heavenly Father, I want to know You more. I want to feel Your presence. Teach me Thy ways that I may dwell in the house of the Lord forever. Amen.

LORD, HELP!

"LORD, help!" they cried in their trouble, and he saved them from their distress. He calmed the storm to a whisper and stilled the waves. What a blessing was that stillness as he brought them safely into harbor!

PSALM 107:28–30 NLT

Samuel Morse, the father of modern communication, said, "The only gleam of hope, and I cannot underrate it, is from confidence in God. When I look upward it calms any apprehension for the future, and I seem to hear a voice saying: 'If I clothe the lilies of the field, shall I not also clothe you?' Here is my strong confidence, and I will wait patiently for the direction of Providence." The answer to your prayer does not depend on you. Your expressions of your heart spoken to your Father bring Him onto the scene for any reason you need Him.

Father, thank You for hearing my prayers.
I know that You are always near to me and You
answer my heart's cry. Help me to come to You
first instead of trying to do things on my own.

ENCOURAGE ONE ANOTHER

Therefore encourage one another and build each other up, just as in fact you are doing.

1 THESSALONIANS 5:11 NIV

Encouragement is more than words. It is also valuing, being tolerant of, serving, and praying for one another. It is looking for what is good and strong in a person and celebrating it. Encouragement means sincerely forgiving and asking for forgiveness, recognizing someone's weaknesses and holding out a helping hand, giving humbly while building someone up, helping others to hope in the Lord, and praying that God will encourage them in ways that you cannot.

Whom will you encourage today?

Heavenly Father, open my eyes to those who need encouragement. Show me how I can help. Amen.

WALK A MILE IN THE MASTER'S SHOES

For this very reason also, applying all diligence, in your faith supply moral excellence, and in your moral excellence, knowledge.

2 PETER 1:5 NASB

God, in His infinite grace and mercy, knows we'll stumble. We can place our hope in Him with confidence He'll understand. He's not there with a "giant thumb" to squash us as we toddle along, new in our spiritual walk. He doesn't look for opportunities to say, "Aha, you messed up!" Quite the contrary: He encourages us with His Word. As we grow and learn with the aid of the Spirit, our lives will also reflect more of Him. And as we grow ever more sure footed, we'll reach our destination—to be like our Father.

Gracious Lord, thank You for Your ever-present guidance. Amen.

LINKING HEARTS WITH GOD

"You will receive power when the Holy Spirit comes on you; and you will be my witnesses. . .to the ends of the earth."

ACTS 1:8 NIV

God knows our hearts. He knows what we need to make it through a day. So in His kindness, He gave us a gift in the form of the Holy Spirit. As a counselor, a comforter, and a friend, the Holy Spirit acts as our inner compass. He upholds us when times are hard and helps us hear God's directions. When the path of obedience grows dark, the Spirit floods it with light. What revelation! He lives within us. Therefore, our prayers are lifted to the Father, to the very throne of God. Whatever petitions we have, we may rest assured they are heard.

Father God, how blessed I am to come into Your presence. Help me, Father, when I am weak. Guide me this day. Amen.

BREATH OF LIFE

He heals the brokenhearted and binds up their wounds [curing their pains and their sorrows].

PSALM 147:3 AMPC

When your life brings disappointment, hurt, and pain that are almost unbearable, remember that you serve the one who heals hearts. He knows you best and loves you most. When the wind is knocked out of you and you feel like there is no oxygen left in the room, let God provide you with the air you need to breathe. Breathe out a prayer to Him and breathe in His peace and comfort today.

Lord, be my breath of life, today and always.

BUILDING TRUST

Trust in the Lord with all your heart and lean not on your own understanding; in all your ways submit to him, and he will make your paths straight.

Proverbs 3:5–6 NIV

Placing our trust in a loving heavenly Father can sometimes feel like stepping off a precipice. Perhaps it is because we can't see God. Trust is not easily attained. It comes once you have built a record with another over a period of time. It involves letting go and knowing you will be caught. In order to trust God, we must step out in faith. Challenge yourself to trust God with one detail in your life each day. Build that trust pattern and watch Him work. He will not let you down.

Father, I release my hold on my life and trust in You. Amen.

THE GIFT OF ENCOURAGEMENT

We have different gifts. . .if it is to encourage, then give encouragement.

ROMANS 12:6–8 NIV

Paul spoke of encouraging as a God-given desire to proclaim God's Word in such a way that it touches hearts to move them to receive the gospel. Encouragement is a vital part to witnessing because encouragement is doused with God's love. For the believer, it stimulates our faith to produce a deeper commitment to Christ. It brings hope to the disheartened or defeated soul. It restores hope. How will you know your spiritual gift? Ask God and then follow the desires He places on your heart.

Father, help me tune in to the needs of those around me so that I might encourage them for the gospel's sake, for Your glory, and for their good.

STANDING IN THE LIGHT

Though I have fallen, I will rise. Though I sit in darkness, the LORD will be my light.

MICAH 7:8 NIV

With God, we know the low times aren't the end of our story. We may fall down, but He will lift us up. We may feel surrounded by darkness on every side, but He will be our light, guiding the way and showing us which step to take next. No matter where we are, what we've done, or what we're facing, God is our rescuer, our Savior, and our friend. God's children always have a future and a hope.

Dear Father, thank You for giving me confidence in a future filled with good things. When I'm down, remind me to trust in Your love. Thank You for lifting me out of darkness to stand in Your light.

GOD'S PROMISES BRING HOPE

"For I know the plans I have for you. . .
plans to prosper you and not to harm you,
plans to give you hope and a future."

JEREMIAH 29:11 NIV

The writer of the well-known hymn, "It Is Well with My Soul," penned those words at the most grief-stricken time of his life after his four children were tragically killed at sea. His undaunted faith remained because he believed in a God who was bigger than the tragedy he faced. God's promises gave him hope and encouragement. Despite your circumstances, God has a plan for you, one that will give you encouragement and hope and a brighter future.

Father, may I always say "it is well with my soul,"
knowing Your promises are true and I
can trust You no matter what.

THE END OF YOUR ROPE

Do not be far from me, for trouble is near and there is no one to help.

PSALM 22:11 NIV

The late youth evangelist Dave Busby said, "The end of your rope is God's permanent address." Jesus reaches down and wraps you in His loving arms when you call to Him for help. The Bible tells us that He is close to the brokenhearted (Psalm 34:18). We may not have the answers we are looking for here in this life, but we can be sure of this: God sees your pain and loves you desperately. Call to Him in times of trouble. If you feel that you're at the end of your rope, look up! His mighty hand is reaching toward you.

Heavenly Father, I feel alone and afraid. Surround me with Your love and give me peace.

I GROW WEARY

But those who wait for the Lord [who expect,
look for, and hope in Him] shall change and renew
their strength and power; they shall lift their wings
and mount up [close to God] as eagles [mount up
to the sun]; they shall run and not be weary,
they shall walk and not faint or become tired.

Isaiah 40:31 AMPC

As long as we are warring inside, we will not find rest. We must find out what Jesus wants for our lives and then obey. Feasting on His Word and learning more about Him will give us the direction we need and the ability to trust. It is only when we understand our salvation and surrender that we can come to Him, unencumbered by guilt or fear, and lay our head on His chest. Safe within His embrace, we can rest.

Father, I am weary and need Your refreshing
Spirit to guide me. I trust in You. Amen.

EVERLASTING LIGHT

In Him was life and that life was the light of all mankind. The light shines in the darkness, and the darkness has not overcome it.

JOHN 1:4–5 NIV

Jesus is the light of the world who holds out wonderful hope for us. Set your prayer life to start with praise and adoration of the King of kings. Lift your voice in song, or read out loud from the Word. The light will eliminate the darkness every time. Keep your heart and mind set on Him as you walk through the day. Give praise for every little thing; nothing is too small for God. A grateful heart and constant praise will bring the light into your day.

Dear Lord, how we love You. We trust in You this day to lead us on the right path lit with Your light. Amen.

HIS STEADY HAND

The Lord makes firm the steps of the one who delights in him; though he may stumble, he will not fall, for the Lord upholds him with his hand.

Psalm 37:23–24 NIV

The Lord knows there are times when we will stumble. We may even backslide into the very activity that caused us to call on the Lord for salvation in the first place. But His Word assures us His love is eternal, and when we cry out to Him, He will hear. Do not be discouraged with those stumbling blocks in your path, because the Lord is with you always. Scripture tells us we are in the palm of His hand. Hope is found in the Lord. He delights in us and wants the very best for us because of His perfect love.

Lord God, the cross was necessary for sinners like me. I thank You that You loved me enough to choose me, and I accepted the free gift of salvation. Amen.

I GIVE UP

God so loved the world that he gave his one and only Son, that whoever believes in him shall not perish but have eternal life.

John 3:16 NIV

Our Creator God cares enough about us to delve into our everyday lives and help us. Through the Holy Spirit within, God's gentle hand of direction will sustain each of us, enabling us to grow closer to our Father. The closer we grow, the more like Him we desire to be. Then His influence spreads through us to others. When we surrender, He is able to use our lives and enrich others. What a powerful message: Give up and give more!

Lord, thank You for loving us despite our frailties. What an encouragement to me today. Amen.

OPEN THE BOOK

For everything that was written in the past was written to teach us, so that through endurance taught in the scriptures and the encouragement they provide we might have hope.

ROMANS 15:4 NIV

Life is tough. We get discouraged and, at times, disheartened to the point of such despair that it's hard to recover. Reading *all* of God's Word is paramount. It is the source of hope, peace, encouragement, salvation, and so much more. It moves people to take action while diminishing depression and discouragement. As the writer of Hebrews put it, "For the word of God is alive and active" and is "sharper than any double-edged sword." (Hebrews 4:12). Need some encouragement? Open the Book.

Lord, help me read Your Word consistently to empower me with the hope and encouragement I need.

FULL REDEMPTION AND LOVE

Israel, put your hope in the LORD, for with the LORD is unfailing love and with him is full redemption.

PSALM 130:7 NIV

The Bible tells us that God removes our sins as far as the east is from the west (Psalm 103:12) and that He remembers our sin no more (Isaiah 43:25; Hebrews 8:12). It's so important to confess your sins to the Lord as soon as you feel convicted and then turn from them and move in a right direction. There is no reason to hang your head in shame over sins of the past. Don't allow the devil to speak lies into your life. You have full redemption through Jesus Christ!

Dear Jesus, I confess my sin to You. Thank You for blotting out each mistake and not holding anything against me. Help me to make right choices through the power of Your Spirit inside me.

PASS IT ON!

After the usual readings from the books of Moses and the prophets, those in charge of the service sent them this message: "Brothers, if you have any word of encouragement for the people, come and give it."

ACTS 13:15 NLT

Encouragement brings hope. Have you ever received a word from someone that instantly lifted your spirit? Did you receive a bit of good news or something that diminished your negative outlook? Perhaps a particular conversation helped to bring your problems into perspective. Paul passed on encouragement and many benefited. So the next time you're encouraged, pass it on! You may never know how your words or actions may benefit someone else.

Lord, thank You for the wellspring of encouragement through Your Holy Word.

HE WON'T LET YOU DOWN

I tell you that Christ has become a servant of the Jews on behalf of God's truth, so that the promises made to the patriarchs might be confirmed.

ROMANS 15:8 NIV

Everyone has been hurt at one time or another by a broken promise. When that happens, it is best to forgive and go on. People are just people. They mess up. But there is one who will never break His promises to us—our heavenly Father. We can safely place our hope in Him. Choose to place your hope in God's promises. You won't be discouraged by time—God's timing is always perfect. You won't be discouraged by circumstances—God can change everything in a heartbeat. He is faithful.

Lord, I choose this day to place my trust in You, for I know You're the one, true constant. Amen.

BRINGING US TO COMPLETION

Being confident of this, that he who began a good work in you will carry it on to completion until the day of Christ Jesus.

PHILIPPIANS 1:6 NIV

No matter how many times we fail, no matter how many times we mess up, we know God hasn't written us off. He's still working on us. He still loves us. Those of us who have been adopted into God's family through believing in His Son, Jesus Christ, can be confident that God won't give up on us. No matter how messed up our lives may seem, He will continue working in us until His plan is fulfilled and we stand before Him, perfect and complete.

Dear Father, thank You for not giving up on me. Help me to cooperate with Your process of fulfilling Your purpose in me.

STRENGTH IN THE LORD

The Lord is my light and my salvation—whom shall I fear? The Lord is the stronghold of my life—of whom shall I be afraid?

Psalm 27:1 NIV

At times, this world can be a tough, unfair, lonely place. Since the fall of man in the garden, things have not been as God originally intended. The Bible assures us that we will face trials in this life, but it also exclaims that we are more than conquerors through Christ who is in us! When you find yourself up against a tribulation that seems insurmountable, *look up*. Christ is there. He goes before you, stands with you, and is backing you up in your time of need. You may lose everyone and everything else in this life, but nothing has the power to separate you from the love of Christ. Nothing.

Jesus, I cling to the hope I have in You. You are my rock, my stronghold, my defense. I will not fear, for You are with me always. Amen.

THANKFUL, THANKFUL HEART

I will praise you, Lord, with all my heart.
I will tell all the miracles you have done.

Psalm 9:1 NCV

When you choose to approach life from the positive side, you can find thankfulness in most of life's circumstances. It completely changes your outlook, your attitude, and your countenance. God wants to bless you. When you are tempted to feel sorry for yourself or to blame others or God for difficulties, push Pause. Take a moment and rewind your life. Look back and count the blessings that God has given you. As you remind yourself of all He has done for you and in you, it will bring change to your attitude and give you hope in the situation you're facing. Count your blessings today.

Lord, I am thankful for my life and all You have done for me. When life happens, help me to respond to it in a healthy, positive way. Remind me to look to You and trust You to carry me through life's challenges.

WHAT IF?

The Lord will keep you from all harm—
he will watch over your life.

Psalm 121:7 NIV

Feeling safe and secure rests not in the world or in other human beings but with God alone. He is a Christian's help and hope in every frightening situation. He promises to provide peace to everyone who puts their faith and trust in Him. What are you afraid of today? Allow God to encourage you. Trust Him to bring you through it and to give you peace.

Dear Lord, hear my prayers, soothe me with
Your words, and give me peace. Amen.

SHOUTS OF JOY

"He will yet fill your mouth with laughter and your lips with shouts of joy."

JOB 8:21 NIV

Do you remember the last time you laughed till you cried? For many of us, it's been far too long. Stress tends to steal our joy, leaving us humorless and oh-so-serious. But lightness and fun haven't disappeared forever. They may be buried beneath the snow of a long, wintery life season, but spring is coming. Laughter will bloom again, and our hearts will soar as our lips shout with joy. Grasp that hope!

Father God, thank You for the hope of joy. I know that because I trust in You, as sure as spring follows winter, joy will again bloom in my heart.

GRANTER OF DREAMS

Hope deferred makes the heart sick,
but a dream fulfilled is a tree of life.
PROVERBS 13:12 NLT

As a teenager, I dreamed of one day writing a book. But life intervened, and I became a wife, mother, occupational therapist, and piano teacher. My writing dream was shelved. Twenty-five years later, after my youngest chick flew the coop, God's still, small voice whispered, "It's time." Within five years, the granter of dreams delivered over seventy articles and nine book contracts. What's your dream? Be brave and take the first step.

Heavenly Father, please give me courage so that I will have the confidence to take the first step in following the dreams You planted deep within my heart.

EVERYDAY BLESSINGS

*But the eyes of the LORD are on those who fear him,
on those whose hope is in his unfailing love.*

PSALM 33:18 NIV

The Lord of all creation is watching our every moment and wants to fill us with His joy. He often interrupts our lives with His blessings: butterflies dancing in sunbeams, dew-touched spiderwebs, cotton-candy clouds, and glorious crimson sunsets. The beauty of His creation reassures us of His unfailing love and fills us with hope. But it is up to us to take the time to notice.

Dear heavenly Father, the next time I spot butterflies dancing in sunbeams, please remind me to whisper a quick thank-you for Your amazing creation.

MY REFUGE

God is our refuge and strength,
always ready to help in times of trouble.

PSALM 46:1 NLT

What is your quiet place? The place you go to get away from the fray, to chill out, think, regroup, and gain perspective? Mine is a hammock nestled beneath a canopy of oaks in my backyard. . .nobody around but birds, squirrels, an occasional wasp, God, and me. There I can pour out my heart to my Lord, hear His comforting voice, and feel His strength refresh me. We all need a quiet place. God, our refuge, will meet us there.

Father, thank You for my special place. . .the place I love to go and spend time in Your presence. Amen.

A LITTLE GOES A LONG WAY

"The LORD our God has allowed a few of us to survive as a remnant."

EZRA 9:8 NLT

Remnants. Useless by most standards, but God is in the business of using tiny slivers of what's left to do mighty things. Nehemiah rebuilt the fallen walls of Jerusalem with a remnant of Israel; Noah's three sons repopulated the earth after the flood; four slave boys—Daniel, Shadrach, Meshach, and Abednego—kept faith alive for an entire nation. When it feels as if bits and pieces are all that has survived of your hope, remember how much God can accomplish with remnants!

Father God, thank You for proving that there is hope. . .even in the remnants! Amen.

INCREASING VISIBILITY

"Where then is my hope?"

JOB 17:15 NIV

On hectic days when fatigue takes its toll, when we feel like cornless husks, hope disappears. When hurting people hurt people and we're in the line of fire, hope vanishes. When ideas fizzle, efforts fail, when we throw the spaghetti against the wall and nothing sticks, hope seems lost. But we must remember it's only temporary. The mountaintop isn't gone just because it's obscured by fog. Visibility will improve tomorrow and hope will rise.

God of Hope, I am thankful to know You. . .and to trust that because of You, hope will rise. Amen.

LORD OF THE DANCE

Remember your promise to me; it is my only hope.

PSALM 119:49 NLT

The Bible contains many promises from God: He will protect us (Proverbs 1:33), comfort us (2 Corinthians 1:5), help in our times of trouble (Psalm 46:1), and encourage us (Isaiah 40:29). The word *encourage* comes from the root phrase "to inspire courage." Like an earthly father encouraging his daughter from backstage as her steps falter during her dance recital, our Papa God wants to inspire courage in us, if we'll only look to Him.

Promise keeper, You are the one true source of courage. Thank You for Your promises and for giving me courage when I need it most.

SMILING IN THE DARKNESS

"The hopes of the godless evaporate."

JOB 8:13 NLT

Hope isn't just an emotion; it's a perspective, a discipline, a way of life. It's a journey of choice. We must learn to override those messages of discouragement, despair, and fear that assault us in times of trouble and press toward the light. Hope is smiling in the darkness. It's confidence that faith in God's sovereignty amounts to something. . . something life changing, lifesaving, and eternal.

Father God, help me smile through the darkness today. Thank You for hope. Amen.

SMALL BUT MIGHTY

"He has. . .exalted the humble."

LUKE 1:52 NLT

God delights in making small things great. He's in the business of taking scrap-heap people and turning them into treasures: Noah (the laughingstock of his city), Moses (stuttering shepherd turned national leader), David (smallest among the big and powerful), Sarah (old and childless), Mary (poor teenager), Rahab (harlot turned faith-filled ancestor of Jesus). So you and I can rejoice with hope! Let us glory in our smallness!

I feel so very small today, God. Please remind me that because I am Yours, I am worthy. And that's all that matters!

KEEP BREATHING, SISTER!

As long as we are alive, we still have hope,
just as a live dog is better off than a dead lion.
ECCLESIASTES 9:4 CEV

Isn't this a tremendous scripture? At first glance, the ending elicits a chuckle. But consider the truth it contains: Regardless of how powerful, regal, or intimidating a lion is, when he's dead, he's dead. But the living—you and I—still have hope. Limitless possibilities! Hope for today and for the future. Although we may be as lowly dogs, fresh, juicy bones abound. As long as we're breathing, it's not too late!

God of possibilities, remind me that it's never too late
as long as I'm breathing. Because of You, I have hope!

JETS AND SUBMARINES

No power in the sky above or in the earth below …will ever be able to separate us from the love of God that is revealed in Christ Jesus our Lord.

ROMANS 8:39 NLT

Have you ever been diving amid the spectacular array of vivid color and teeming life in the silent world under the sea? Painted fish of rainbow hues are backlit by diffused sunbeams. Multitextured coral dot the gleaming white sand. You honestly feel as if you're in another world. But every world is God's world. He soars above the clouds with us and spans the depths of the seas. Nothing can separate us from His love.

Your love amazes me, Father. Just when I find myself questioning how You could possibly love me so much, I am reminded of the precious promises of Your Word.

GO FOR IT

When everything was hopeless,
Abraham believed anyway, deciding to
live. . .on what God said he would do.

ROMANS 4:18 MSG

"You can't do that. It's impossible." Have you ever been told this? Or just thought it because of fear or a previous experience with failure? This world is full of those who discourage rather than encourage. If we believe them, we'll never do anything. But if we, like Abraham, believe that God has called us for a particular purpose, we'll go for it despite our track records. Past failure doesn't dictate future failure. If God wills it, He fulfills it.

Help me to have the faith of Abraham,
Father God. . .to believe anyway!

CAN YOU HEAR ME NOW?

But as for me, I watch in hope for the LORD,
I wait for God my Savior; my God will hear me.

MICAH 7:7 NIV

If there's anything more frustrating than waiting for someone who never shows, it's trying to talk to someone who isn't listening. It's as if they have plugged their ears and nothing penetrates. Mothers are well acquainted with this exercise in futility, as are wives, daughters, and sisters. But the Bible tells us that God hears us when we talk to Him. He shows up when we wait for Him. He will not disappoint us.

When I talk, Lord, I know You will listen.
You will never let me down.

A NEW TOMORROW

Rahab the prostitute. . .Joshua spared. . .
because she hid the messengers whom
Joshua sent to spy out Jericho.

JOSHUA 6:25 NASB

Rahab was the unlikeliest of heroes: a prostitute who sold her body in the darkest shadows. Yet she was the very person God chose to fulfill His prophecy. How astoundingly freeing! Especially for those of us ashamed of our past. God loved Rahab for who she was—not what she did. Rahab is proof that God can and will use anyone for His higher purposes. Anyone. . .even you and me.

When I feel absolutely useless, God, remind me of Rahab's story. If you could use Rahab for Your purposes, You can certainly use me!

CHERISHED DESIRE

God our Father loves us. . .and has given us eternal comfort and a wonderful hope.

2 THESSALONIANS 2:16 CEV

Webster's definition of *hope*: "to cherish a desire with anticipation." In other words, yearning for something wonderful you expect to occur. Our hope in Christ is not just yearning for something wonderful, as in "I hope for a sunny beach day." It's a deep trust with roots that extend from the beginning of time to the infinite future. Our hope is not just the anticipation of heaven, but the expectation of a fulfilling life walking beside our Creator and best friend.

Dear heavenly Father, I want to journey through life in hopeful expectation—always anticipating You'll work in wonderful ways!

SEEKING AN OASIS

He turns a wilderness into a pool of water
and a dry land into springs of water.
PSALM 107:35 NASB

The wilderness of Israel is truly a barren wasteland—nothing but rocks and parched sand stretching as far as the distant horizon. The life-and-death contrast between stark desert and pools of oasis water is startling. Our lives can feel parched too. Colorless. Devoid of life. But God has the power to transform desert lives into gurgling, spring-of-water lives. Ask Him to bubble up springs of hope within you today.

When I am feeling parched, Jesus, I trust
You'll create a peaceful oasis in my soul.
Envelop my spirit in Your hope, Lord.

FEEL THE LOVE

Long before he laid down earth's foundations,
he had us in mind, had settled on us as the focus of
his love, to be made whole and holy by his love.

EPHESIANS 1:4 MSG

Need a boost of hope today? Read this passage aloud, inserting your name for each "us." Wow! Doesn't that bring home the message of God's incredible, extravagant, and customized love for you? I am the focus of His love, and I bask in the hope of healing, wholeness, and holiness His individualized attention brings. You too, dear sister, are His focus. Allow yourself to feel the love today.

Long before You laid down earth's foundations,
You had me in mind, had settled on me as the
focus of Your love, to be made whole and holy
by Your love. Thank You, Jesus! Amen.

PERMISSION TO MOURN

When I heard this, I sat down on the ground and cried. Then for several days, I mourned; I went without eating to show my sorrow, and I prayed.

NEHEMIAH 1:4 CEV

Bad news. When it arrives, what's your reaction? Do you scream? Fall apart? Run away? Nehemiah's response to bad news is a model for us. First, he vented his sorrow. It's okay to cry and mourn. Christians suffer pain like everyone else—only we know the source of inner healing. Disguising our struggle doesn't make us look more spiritual. . .just less real. Like Nehemiah, our next step is to turn to the only true source of help and comfort.

Thank You for being big enough, God, to carry my sorrow. I am thankful that with You, I can always be real. . .sharing my every thought and emotion. And You love me still!

PEBBLES

"I will give you a new heart and put a new spirit within you; and I will remove the heart of stone from your flesh and give you a heart of flesh."

EZEKIEL 36:26 NASB

So many things can harden our hearts: overwhelming loss; shattered dreams; even scar tissue from broken hearts, disillusionment, and disappointment. To avoid pain, we simply turn off feelings. Our hearts become petrified rock—heavy, cold, and rigid. But God can crack our hearts of stone from the inside out and replace that miserable pile of pebbles with soft, feeling hearts of flesh. The amazing result is a brand-new, hope-filled spirit.

God, please take my hard heart and make it soft again. Renew my spirit with Your hope. Transform me from the inside out! Amen.

DO A LITTLE DANCE

Then Miriam. . .took a tambourine and led all the women as they played their tambourines and danced.

EXODUS 15:20 NLT

Can you imagine the enormous celebration that broke out among the children of Israel when God miraculously saved them from Pharaoh's army? Even dignified prophetess Miriam grabbed her tambourine and cut loose with her girlfriends. Despite adverse circumstances, she heard God's music and did His dance. Isn't that our goal today? To hear God's music above the world's cacophony and do His dance as we recognize everyday miracles in our lives?

Make me aware of Your everyday miracles, Father. Help me to listen closely for Your music so I can join in the dance. Amen.

UP IS THE ONLY OUT

Let them lie face down in the dust,
for there may be hope at last.
LAMENTATIONS 3:29 NLT

The Old Testament custom for grieving people was to lie prostrate and cover themselves with ashes. Perhaps the thought was that when you're wallowing in the dust, at least you can't descend any further. There's an element of hope in knowing that there's only one way to go—up. If a recent loss has you sprawled in the dust, know that God doesn't waste pain in our lives. He will use it for some redeeming purpose.

Help me to recognize the purpose in my pain, Father.
I know You have a plan for my life—and that Your
plans are good. I trust You, Father. Amen.

HOME

"But we will devote ourselves to prayer and to the ministry of the word."

ACTS 6:4 NASB

As busy women, we've found out the hard way that we can't do everything. Heaven knows we've tried, but the truth has found us out: Superwoman is a myth. So we must make priorities and focus on the most important. Prayer and God's Word should be our faith priorities. If we only do as much as we can do, then God will take over and do what only He can do. He's got our backs, girls!

I know I can't do it all, God. I find comfort in knowing that if I put my faith in You wholeheartedly, You will always help me prioritize my to-do list and get the R&R I need.

SPROUTS

"For there is hope for a tree, when it is cut down, that it will sprout again."

JOB 14:7 NASB

Have you ever battled a stubborn tree? You know, one you can saw off at the ground but the tenacious thing keeps sprouting new growth from the roots? You have to admire the resiliency of that life force, struggling in its refusal to give up. That's hope in a nutshell, sisters. We must believe, even as stumps, that we will eventually become majestic, towering evergreens if we just keep sending out those sprouts.

Father God, help me continue to hope that I will grow into the woman You created me to be—just like the majestic, towering evergreen.

MAKEOVER

Since I was worse than anyone else, God had mercy on me and let me be an example of the endless patience of Christ Jesus.

1 TIMOTHY 1:16 CEV

Saul was a Jesus hater. He went out of his way to hunt down believers to torture, imprison, and kill. Yet Christ tracked him down and confronted him in a blinding light on a dusty road. Saul's past no longer mattered. Previous sins were forgiven and forgotten. He was given a fresh start. A life makeover. We, too, are offered a life makeover. Christ offers to create a beautiful new image of Himself in us, unblemished and wrinkle-free.

Thank You for new beginnings and fresh starts, God. You have erased my sins, and now I walk free in Your unending grace!

SNIPPETS OF HOPE

I also pray that you will understand the incredible greatness of God's power for us who believe him.

EPHESIANS 1:19 NLT

Daydreams are snippets of hope for our souls—yearnings for something better, something more exciting, something that lifts our spirits. Some dreams are mere fancy, but others are meant to last a lifetime because God embedded them in our hearts. It's when we lose sight of those dreams that hope dies. But God offers us access to His almighty power— the very same greatness that brought His Son back from the dead. What greater hope is there?

Thank You for the dreams you wove into my heart, Father God. Please help me keep those dreams for the future alive. Amen.

EASY AS ABC

God has done all this, so that we will look for him and reach out and find him. He isn't far from any of us.

ACTS 17:27 CEV

God is near. But we must reach out for Him. There's a line that we choose to cross, a specific action we take. We can't ooze into the kingdom of God; it's an intentional decision. It's simple, really—as simple as ABC. A is Admitting we're sinful and in need of a Savior. B is Believing that Jesus died for our sins and rose from the grave. C is Committing our lives to Him. Life everlasting is then ours.

God, You are always within reach. For that,
I am so very thankful. I look forward to
eternal life in Your presence. Amen.

AIM HIGH

My aim is to raise hopes by pointing the way to life without end.

TITUS 1:2 MSG

No woman is an island. We're more like peninsulas. Although we sometimes feel isolated, we're connected to one another by the roots of womanhood. We're all in this together, girls. As we look around, we can't help but see sisters who need a hand, a warm smile, a caring touch. And especially hope. People need hope, and if we know the Lord—the source of eternal hope—it's up to us to point the way through love.

I have so many women in my life who are constant reminders of the one eternal source of hope—YOU, Father God. Thank You for placing these beautiful women in my life.

FILL 'ER UP

"What strength do I have, that I should still hope?"

JOB 6:11 NIV

Run, rush, hurry, dash—a typical American woman's day. It's easy to identify with David's lament in Psalm 22:14 (NASB): "I am poured out like water. . .my heart is like wax; it is melted within me." Translation: I'm pooped; I'm numb; I'm drained dry. When we are at the end of our strength, God doesn't want us to lose hope or sight of the refilling He can provide if we only lift our empty cups to Him.

Fill me up, Lord! I need Your heavenly presence. . .Your strength. . .Your comfort. Thank You for the hope you provide in the daily-ness of life!

LAUGH A RAINBOW

"When I see the rainbow in the clouds,
I will remember the eternal covenant between
God and every living creature on earth."
GENESIS 9:16 NLT

Ever feel like a cloud is hanging over your head? Sometimes the cloud darkens to the color of bruises, and we're deluged with cold rain that seems to have no end. When you're in the midst of one of life's thunderstorms, tape this saying to your mirror: "Cry a river, laugh a rainbow." The rainbow, the symbol of hope that God gave Noah after the flood, reminds us even today that every storm will eventually pass.

The rainbows you place in the sky after a storm are lovely reminders of the hope we have in You, God. Because of You, I know that the storms of life are only temporary. . .and You will bring beauty from the storms.

HE WILL COME

Do not snatch your word of truth from me,
for your regulations are my only hope.
Psalm 119:43 NLT

Bibles wear and tear. Papers get discarded. Hard drives crash. But memorizing scripture assures us that God's Word will never be lost. His truth will always be at our disposal, any moment of the day or night when we need a word of encouragement, guidance, or hope. Like a phone call from heaven, our Father communicates to us via scripture implanted in our hearts. But it is up to us to build the signal tower.

Your Word is a never-ending source of hope in my life. When troubles come, I find comfort, peace, strength, love. . .whatever my soul thirsts for, I know I will find it in the Bible.

HOW SHOULD I TALK TO GOD?

"This, then, is how you should pray: 'Our Father in heaven, hallowed be your name, your kingdom come, your will be done, on earth as it is in heaven. Give us today our daily bread. And forgive us our debts, as we also have forgiven our debtors. And lead us not into temptation, but deliver us from the evil one.'"

MATTHEW 6:9–13 NIV

Jesus gave us an example of how to pray in His famous petition that was recorded in Matthew 6:9–13. We don't need to suffer with an anxious heart or feel ensnared by this world with no one to hear our cry for help. We can talk to God, right now, and He will listen. The act of prayer is as simple as launching a boat into the Sea of Galilee, but it's as miraculous as walking on water.

God, how wonderful it is that You hear me when I call out to You, and that You answer with exactly what I need. Amen.

GOD IS DOING SOMETHING NEW

"See, I am doing a new thing! Now it springs up; do you not perceive it? I am making a way in the wilderness and streams in the wasteland."

ISAIAH 43:19 NIV

Imagine that desert, dry and barren—with no hope of even a cactus flower to bloom—suddenly coming to life with bubbling pools of pure water. That is what God promises us. He is doing something new in our lives. He is making a path through what feels impassable, and He will command a stream to flow through the wilderness of our pasts, places where we had only known the wasteland of sin and a landscape of despair. Have faith and bring your empty buckets to the stream.

Father, thank You for Your provision, hope, and joy. Without You, life is dry and hostile. Come into my life and quench my thirst. You are the only one who can fulfill me. Amen.

WHICH WAY DO I GO?

I will instruct you and teach you in the way you should go; I will counsel you with my loving eye on you.

PSALM 32:8 NIV

God says, "I will instruct you and teach you in the way you should go; I will counsel you with my loving eye on you." That is truly what we need in a noisy world that may offer little reliable or usable advice. God not only promises to guide us, to teach us the way we should go, but He plans on doing it with a loving eye on us. For the most loving counsel, listen to the voice of God. He's talking to you, and He has something important to say that will change your life.

Wonderful Counselor, help me to be receptive to Your voice and to always trust in Your guidance. Amen.

DIVINE IMAGININGS AND SUBLIME ASPIRATIONS

He has made everything beautiful in its time.
He has also set eternity in the human heart.

ECCLESIASTES 3:11 NIV

Let's join hands. Let's celebrate. God has made everything beautiful in its time. He has also set eternity in the human heart. Never sit in the gutter when the steps of paradise are at your feet! So, widen your scope. See beauty in all things great and small. Soar free. Imagine beyond the ordinary. Love large. Forgive lavishly. Hope always. Expect a miracle.

Father, give me a contagious enthusiasm for life.
You have given me everything I need. Amen.

LIVING THE "WHAT-IF" BLUES

And we know that in all things God works for the good of those who love him, who have been called according to his purpose.

ROMANS 8:28 NIV

All of life's "not knowing" can prompt a lot of "what-ifs." Pray for wisdom and guidance, knowing that God will give them to you freely and lovingly. But if you still take a wrong turn, embrace His promise that He will work all things for good for those who love Him. Hard to imagine, but the Lord really does mean "all things." Praying and embracing His promises will go a long way in keeping you on the right road, as well as easing those "what-if" blues.

God, I'm so grateful You can turn evil into good and sorrow into joy. Amen.

THE WORRIER'S PSALM

Do not fret.

PSALM 37:1 NIV

Instead of fretting, delight in the Lord, and He will give you all your heart's desires. Especially if one of those desires is to be free from fretting. And even if you've prayed, breathed, and tried to relax, and the worries still come, like houseflies that just refuse to find their way back out the screen, then don't fret about fretting. Trust. Commit. Be still. Wait. Refrain. Turn. Give generously. Lend freely. Do good. Hope. Consider. Observe. Seek peace. Just don't fret.

Dear God, You know our hearts and the worries that prey on our minds. Please help us to stay busy doing good and to grow in trust and patience. Please help us to let go of control we never had to start with. Amen.

THE ANSWER IS NO ONE

The Lord is my light and my salvation—whom shall I fear?

Psalm 27:1 NIV

When you accept Christ as your Savior, you get certain things in return. You get an understanding of good and evil—and you get the knowledge that you are on the side of good. You get a clearer vision of the darkness in your life—and you get a friend who is always with you, no matter how dark things seem to be. And you get peace—through knowing your place before God. That you stand in His grace, blameless and pure, and you have a place in heaven created just for you. A place no one can take away.

Dear Jesus, help me to feel You at my side. Amen.

PLANTING

I planted the seed, Apollos watered it,
but God has been making it grow.
1 CORINTHIANS 3:6 NIV

Have you ever hesitated to engage in a spiritual discussion with a person because you didn't know how he would take it or you felt like you didn't have the time required to build a relationship with him? Of course, in an ideal world, we'd have time to sit and chat with everyone for days, and the coffee would be free. But the fact that our world isn't ideal should not prevent us from planting a seed. You just never know what might happen to it. And that makes for some exciting gardening.

Dear God, thank You for allowing me to work for Your kingdom. Help me to plant more seeds. Amen.

OUR SONG

By day the LORD directs his love, at night his song is with me—a prayer to the God of my life.

PSALM 42:8 NIV

All through the Bible, we find people worshipping God through song. They sing to God about winning battles and the birth of babies. They sing songs of lament and songs of praise, songs sinking with sorrow and songs bouncing with joy. There is, of course, a whole book devoted just to this exercise: Psalms. By day God guides us, and at night He still leaves the doors of communication open. What do you think His song is saying to you? What do you want to sing to Him?

Dear God, help me listen for Your song, and help me find the words to sing praise to You every day. Amen.

OUR GREAT CONTENDER

Do not be far from me, Lord. Awake, and rise to my defense! Contend for me, my God and Lord. Vindicate me in your righteousness, LORD my God.

PSALM 35:22–24 NIV

Our Lord God is the greatest warrior of all time. He is our guide, our leader, our defender, our shield. He is all-powerful, all-knowing, all-mighty, and all good. Why would we ever hesitate to call on Him? Why would we ever think that our own strength could somehow be diminished by being supported by the Creator of the universe? The next time you find yourself facing a battle, don't wait. Don't try to do it on your own. Don't stand up by yourself. Ask God to contend for you.

Almighty God, please defend me from my enemies and help me fight my battles. Amen.

ABOVE ALL

Above all, love each other deeply,
because love covers over a multitude of sins.
1 PETER 4:8 NIV

How deep does your love go? Does it go as far as the distance that grows between two people? Does it cover little insults? Is it deep enough to silence words that should not be said? How deep does your love go? Does it go deep enough to trust? Can it cover over deceit? Does it go deep enough to swallow up betrayal? How deep does Jesus' love go?

Dear Jesus, help me to love as You love. Amen.

MORNING ORDERS

"Have you ever given orders to the morning, or shown the dawn its place, that it might take the earth by the edges and shake the wicked out of it?"

JOB 38:12–13 NIV

God poses many rhetorical questions, all to show the might and wonder and mystery of the Almighty. In these words are some amazing ideas that really cause us to stop and consider who God is. And that is what we should do, especially when we face our worst trials. Stop and consider who God is. That no matter what happens, He will not leave us. And that He alone has the answers for us.

Thank You, God, for providing glimpses of You in Your Word. Amen.

GLUE

He is before all things,
and in him all things hold together.
COLOSSIANS 1:17 NIV

Have you ever felt like your life was falling apart? We need to know that there is someone who is holding us together, even when we feel like falling apart. Jesus has been with us since the beginning. He is "the beginning and the firstborn from among the dead" (verse 18). He can handle our struggles. And He can put us back together again, even if we let everything fall. There is always hope in Him.

Dear Jesus, thank You for being a friend I can always count on. Help me remember to trust You with all the details of my life. Amen.

HE WROTE THEM BOTH

God has made the one as well as the other.

ECCLESIASTES 7:14 NIV

We need to learn to see God's grace, not just in what He does for us but in what He doesn't do. And we need to realize that the bit of the world we see is just one small piece of a very large story. So when we are standing in the middle of the book and the chapter is a sad and dreary one, we need to remember at least these two things: First, there are many pages to come; and second, it is by God's grace we are living this story, good or bad as it may be.

Dear author of my life, help me to remember to trust You to write my story. Amen.

FATHER GOD

You are the helper of the fatherless.

PSALM 10:14 NIV

Some of us were blessed with great fathers. These were men who enriched our lives as role models, trainers, encouragers, supporters, huggers, comforters, and friends. But if your father was never there for you or is now gone, run to your Father God and spend some time with Him. Let Him heal the places in you that are hurting and give you the confidence that comes from the only person in the world who has loved you since before the day you were born—and will continue to love you forever.

Dear Father, hear and bless Your children. Amen.

TO GET THE PRIZE

Everyone who competes in the games goes into strict training.

1 CORINTHIANS 9:25 NIV

We are in the race of life. Time is short, but the days are long. We have a lot to do, and we never know when our life will come to an end. All of us are running to the same finish line. It's important that we run our races in a way that shows we are serious about getting the prize—eternal life with Christ. We need to show that we are running toward something worth sacrificing for. And we need to be prepared for whatever falls in our paths—including other runners.

Dear God, please help me "run in such a way as to get the prize" (1 Corinthians 9:24). Amen.

SEWING UP BROKEN HEARTS

He heals the brokenhearted and binds up their wounds.

PSALM 147:3 NIV

A heart that does not feel cannot be broken. But it also cannot love. And a heart that loves deeply can be wounded deeply. But God is the great healer. And He knows how to heal deeply. God searches our hearts and finds the holes. Then He carefully, over time, joins the pieces together—with new love, care, and understanding. A broken heart will never be the same as an innocent one. It is forever scarred. But with the scarring comes wisdom, and that wisdom can blossom into compassion for others who have been hurt as well.

Dear healer, mend the holes in my heart so I can offer my whole heart to You. Amen.

SHINE

"Those who are wise will shine like the brightness of the heavens, and those who lead many to righteousness, like the stars for ever and ever."

DANIEL 12:3 NIV

The next time you are feeling a little frumpy or gray, a little old and tarnished, thank God for the wisdom you have. Think about the best decisions you made in the past year. Then pick yourself up, put on something shiny (an aluminum foil tiara? A bouquet of silverware?), and take your own photo. Print it out and write beneath it, "I Shine." Then put it somewhere to serve as a reminder that being wise can be beautiful too.

Dear Lord, thank You for allowing me to shine with wisdom. Amen.

HARM FOR GOOD

"You intended to harm me,
but God intended it for good."
GENESIS 50:20 NIV

Instead of feeling entitled to apologies, Joseph wanted redemption in place of revenge. In response to his brothers wanting security, he replied, "Don't be afraid. Am I in the place of God? You intended to harm me, but God intended it for good to accomplish what is now being done, the saving of many lives" (verses 19–20).

Maybe you're in the middle of suffering right now, so deep in it you can't possibly see any good. Take encouragement from Joseph's words. You are not God—you cannot see what He sees. Maybe yet there will be some good that comes out of the harm.

Dear God, help me to trust in Your plans. Amen.

FINISH LINE

I have fought the good fight,
I have finished the race, I have kept the faith.

2 TIMOTHY 4:7 NIV

Paul felt his life was coming to an end. As he wrote to his friend Timothy, he spoke of this. He was not boasting, he was just giving his status report, as it were. Good fight fought? Check. Race finished? Check (well, almost). Faith kept? Check. What's your checklist include? What accomplishments make your list? What goals do you want to be known for achieving? What do you want to do, who do you want to become, before your race is finished? Write them down today. Put a checkbox by each one. Then go and work out your life, faith, and ministry for all you're worth. Godspeed.

Dear Lord, bless the work of my hands and feet.
Make me Your servant so that at the end of my life,
I can look forward to hearing You say, "Well done." Amen.

WOMEN WHO LOVED WELL

Charm is deceptive, and beauty is fleeting.

PROVERBS 31:30 NIV

In the end, it will matter to Jesus, of course, that we knew Him as our friend and Savior, but it will also matter that while we walked this earthly life, we loved well. That we saw a need and met it. That we smiled when we wanted to frown. That we were handier with a cup of cool water than a witty comeback. That we chased after a lost soul faster than we chased after a good time. That we loved other people as ourselves. Those things will matter a great deal, and with the power of the Holy Spirit, all those things are within our grasp. They are also ours to give away. Fully, freely—and daily.

Heavenly Father, help me to focus on cultivating those qualities and virtues that are lasting and will make an eternal impact for Your kingdom. Amen.

THE TREES THAT CATCH THE STORM

Brothers and sisters, I could not address you as people who live by the Spirit but as people who are still worldly—mere infants in Christ. I gave you milk, not solid food, for you were not yet ready for it. Indeed, you are still not ready.

1 CORINTHIANS 3:1–2 NIV

Think of the healthiest trees that shoot up from the forest floor. . .they stretch toward the sun and spread their branches wide. But when the storms of life blow through, many times it's those towering oaks that will catch the brunt of the wind. The last thing the enemy of your soul wants is for you to grow in Christ and His wisdom. So, expect storms, and be watchful and ready. But remember, too, that we can stand strong like the oak trees. We can know peace in the midst of the gale. For Christ is the strength in our branches and the light who gives us life!

Jesus, help me to grow strong in the rich, nourishing soil of Your love and grace. Make me a warrior for Your cause. Amen.

WHAT TO DO WITH FREE WILL

"If you do what is right, will you not be accepted? But if you do not do what is right, sin is crouching at your door; it desires to have you, but you must rule over it."

GENESIS 4:7 NIV

Every single thing we do every minute of the day involves a choice, and everything has a ripple effect. Everything has consequences. What we eat for breakfast. What books we read. What programs we watch on TV. Where we go, what we spend our time and money on. Sin is always crouching at our door, but with the help of the Holy Spirit, we can ask it to leave.

What will your choices be today?

Holy Spirit, guide me in my decisions. Help me to be wise, clearheaded, and motivated by a selfless love for You and others. Amen.

ALL THE LONELY PEOPLE

Be devoted to one another in love.
Honor one another above yourselves.
ROMANS 12:10 NIV

As Christians, let's keep an eye out for those lonely souls, the people who need a smile and a helping hand. Those who need a cup of cool water and a listening ear—who need a friend. Let us open our hearts and homes to them. As the book of Romans reminds us, "Be devoted to one another in love. Honor one another above yourselves." This is God's cure for all the lonely people. Amazingly enough, when we reach out to lessen someone else's lonesomeness, perhaps we will ease our own.

Father, give me the desire to live my life for You and for everyone around me. Deepen and enrich my relationships with family and friends. Amen.

TURNING BONDAGE INTO BALANCE

It is for freedom that Christ has set us free.
Stand firm, then, and do not let yourselves
be burdened again by a yoke of slavery.

GALATIANS 5:1 NIV

The Lord wants us to have a sound mind, which means finding balance in life. How can we be warm, giving, creative, fun, and a light to the world if we are frozen solid in an unmovable block of perfectionism? Let Jesus melt the block of bondage that says, "Never good enough," and let us be able to shout the words, "It is good, and it is finished. Praise God!"

Lord, help me not to be a slave to perfectionism,
but in all things, let me find balance and joy. Amen.

THE TIME IS NOW

But God demonstrates his own love for us in this: While we were still sinners, Christ died for us.

ROMANS 5:8 NIV

In the book of Mark, Jesus said, "The time has come. . . The kingdom of God has come near. Repent and believe the good news!" (1:15). Have you embraced this good news? The kingdom of God has come near to you. Why are you waiting? The time is now. Ask the Lord for forgiveness and be free. Believe in Him as Lord and be made right with God. Accept His grace and live with the Lord for all time. Oh, yes, what a joy—to know love the way it was meant to be!

Thank You, Lord Jesus, that even while I was deep in my sin, You gave up your life so that I might truly live. What a sacrifice. What a Savior! Thank You for Your unfathomable mercy, Your immeasurable love. Amen.

RIGHT PEOPLE, RIGHT PLACE, RIGHT TIME

And so find favor and high esteem
in the sight of God and man.

PROVERBS 3:4 NKJV

God wants you to experience every favor and rich blessing He's prepared. By faith, expect blessing to meet you at every turn. Imagine what your future holds when you become determined to step out to greet it according to God's design. Remain alert and attentive to what God wants to add to your life. Expect the goodness He has planned for you—doors of opportunities are opening for you today!

Lord, thank You for setting favor and blessing
in my path, and help me to expect it wherever
I go and in whatever I do. Amen.

TREMBLING WHILE TRUSTING

And straightway the father of the child cried out, and said with tears, Lord, I believe; help thou mine unbelief.

MARK 9:24 KJV

When the Lord looks at us, what does He see? Do we trust Him enough to be vulnerable? Are we willing to obey even when we are afraid? Do we believe Him?

Do not be afraid to follow Him, and do not let your trembling hold you back. Be willing to take a step of faith. If you are scared, God understands and is compassionate and merciful. Fear does not negate His love for you. Your faith will grow as you trust Him. Let's trust even while trembling.

Dear Lord, help my unbelief. Enable me to trust You even though I may be trembling. Amen.

GET REAL

The Lord says: "These people come near to me with their mouth and honor me with their lips, but their hearts are far from me. Their worship of me is based on merely human rules they have been taught."

ISAIAH 29:13 NIV

The world is full of hypocrites. To be honest, sometimes the church is too—hypocrites who profess to know and honor God, but when it comes right down to it, they are only going through the motions of religion. Their hearts are far from Him. Take the time to find out who God is, what He has done for you, and why He is worthy of your devotion. Following God is not about a bunch of man-made rules. He loves you, He sent His Son to die for you, and He longs to have a deep, personal relationship with you. Get real with God and get real with yourself!

Dear God, reveal Yourself to me. Show me who You are and show me how to live so that I honor You not only with my lips, but with my heart as well. Amen.

EQUIPPED TO DO GOD'S WILL

May the God of peace, who through the blood of the eternal covenant brought back from the dead our Lord Jesus, that great Shepherd of the sheep, equip you with everything good for doing his will, and may he work in us what is pleasing to him, through Jesus Christ, to whom be glory for ever and ever. Amen.

HEBREWS 13:20–21 NIV

Hebrews says God will work in us what is pleasing to Him. When He is at work in you, you may be stretched mentally, emotionally, physically, and spiritually to new places. The good news is that He provides you with everything you need. Like a good football coach wants his team to succeed, God wants His children to receive the blessing of living in His perfect will. You are equipped for the ride!

Father, I ask that You equip me to do Your will in my life.

I THINK I CAN

"Do not be afraid; only believe."

MARK 5:36 NKJV

Take a trip through the Bible and you'll see that those God asked to do the impossible were ordinary people of their day, yet they demonstrated that they believed God saw something in them that they didn't see. He took ordinary men and women and used them to do extraordinary things. When you believe you can do something, your faith goes to work. You rise to the challenge, which enables you to go further than before, to do more than you thought possible. Consider trying something new—if you think you can, you can!

God, I want to have high expectations. I want to do more than most think I can do. Help me to reach higher and do more as You lead me. Amen.

OWNING YOUR FAITH

"But the Helper, the Holy Spirit, whom the Father will send in My name, He will teach you all things, and bring to your remembrance all things that I said to you."

JOHN 14:26 NKJV

Is your faith deeper and stronger than when you first accepted Jesus? While we are responsible for choosing to grow in faith, we can't do it on our own. Jesus promises that the Holy Spirit will teach and guide us if we allow Him to. He will help us remember the spiritual truths we've learned over the years. Fellowship with other Christians also helps us to mature as we share our passions and are encouraged. God wants you to own your faith. Make it real with words and actions.

Jesus, I want to know You intimately.
Help me to mature in my walk with You daily.
Guide my steps as I seek You through Your Word. Amen.

WHAT'S IN YOUR HEART?

Delight thyself also in the Lord: and he shall give thee the desires of thine heart.

Psalm 37:4 KJV

Too many times we look at God's promises as some sort of magic formula. We fail to realize that His promises have more to do with our own relationship with Him. It begins with a heart's desire to live your life in a way that pleases God. Only then will fulfillment of His promises take place.

The promise in Psalm 37:4 isn't intended for personal gain—it is meant to glorify God. God wants to give you the desires of your heart when they line up with His perfect plan. As you delight in Him, His desires will become your desires, and you will be greatly blessed.

Lord, I know You want to give me the desires of my heart. Help me live in a way that makes this possible.

ALL YOU NEED

"For your Maker is your husband—the Lord Almighty is his name—the Holy One of Israel is your Redeemer; he is called the God of all the earth."

Isaiah 54:5 NIV

God is the great "I Am." He is all things that we need. He is our maker. He is our husband. He is the Lord Almighty, the Holy One, the Redeemer, the God of all the earth. . . . He is not a god made of stone or metal. He is not unreachable. He is present. He is near, as close as you will let Him be, and He will meet your needs as no earthly relationship can. Seek the fullness of God in your life. Call upon Him as your Prince of Peace and your King of Glory. He is all that you need—at all times—in all ways.

Oh, Father, be close to me. Fill the empty spots in my heart. Be my husband, my Redeemer, and my best friend. Amen.

MY LIFE

I long for your salvation, LORD, and your law gives me delight. Let me live that I may praise you, and may your laws sustain me.

PSALM 119:174–175 NIV

Can you really do laundry to please God? Can you really go to work to please God? Can you really pay the bills and make dinner to please God? The answer is a resounding *yes*! Doing all the mundane tasks of everyday life with gratitude and praise in your heart for all that He has done for you is living a life of praise. As you worship God through your day-to-day life, He makes clear His plans, goals, and dreams for you.

Dear Father, let me live my life to praise You. Let that be my desire each day. Amen.

NO MATTER WHAT

Be thankful in all circumstances, for this is God's will for you who belong to Christ Jesus.

1 THESSALONIANS 5:18 NLT

Jesus enables us to be thankful, and Jesus is the cause of our thankfulness. *No matter what happens*, we know that Jesus has given up His life to save ours. He has sacrificed Himself on the cross so that we may live life to the fullest. And while "to the fullest" means that we will experience pain as well as joy, we must *always* be thankful—regardless of our circumstances—for the love that we experience in Christ Jesus.

Dear Lord, thank You for Your love. Please let me be thankful, even in the midst of hardships. You have blessed me beyond measure. Amen.

ABIDE IN THE VINE

"I am the vine; you are the branches. If you remain in me and I in you, you will bear much fruit; apart from me you can do nothing."

JOHN 15:5 NIV

The fruit we bear is consistent with Christ's character. Just as apple trees bear apples, we bear spiritual fruit that reflects Him. Spiritual fruit consists of God's qualities: love, joy, peace, patience, kindness, goodness, faithfulness, gentleness, and self-control. The fruit of the spirit cannot be grown by our own efforts. We must remain in the vine.

How do we abide in Him? We acknowledge that our spiritual sustenance comes from the Lord. We spend time with Him. We seek His will and wisdom. We are obedient and follow where He leads. Abide in the vine and be fruitful!

Dear Lord, help me abide in You so that I may produce fruit as a witness to Your life within me. Amen.

GOD CARES FOR YOU

"Consider how the wild flowers grow. They do not labor or spin. Yet I tell you, not even Solomon in all his splendor was dressed like one of these. If that is how God clothes the grass of the field, which is here today, and tomorrow is thrown into the fire, how much more will he clothe you—you of little faith!"

LUKE 12:27–28 NIV

If God makes the flowers, each type unique and beautiful, and if He sends the rain and sun to meet their needs, will He not care for you as well?

He made you. What the Father makes, He loves. And what He loves, He cares for. We were made in His image. Humans are dearer to God than any of His other creations. Rest in Him. Trust Him. Just as He cares for the birds of the air and the flowers of the meadows, God is in the business of taking care of His sons and daughters. Let Him take care of you.

Father, I am amazed by Your creation.
Remind me that I am Your treasured child.
Take care of me today as only You can do. Amen.

SETTING PRIORITIES

Cause me to hear Your lovingkindness in the morning, for in You do I trust; cause me to know the way in which I should walk, for I lift up my soul to You.

PSALM 143:8 NKJV

Twenty-four hours. That's what we all get in a day. Though we often think we don't have time for all we want to do, our Creator deemed twenty-four-hour days sufficient. How do we decide what to devote ourselves to? The wisdom of the psalmist tells us to begin the day by asking to hear the loving voice of the one who made us. We can lay our choices, problems, and conflicts before Him in prayer. He will show us which way to go. Psalm 118:7 (NIV) says, "The LORD is with me; he is my helper." Hold up that full plate of your life to Him, and allow Him to decide what to keep and what to let go.

Lord, make me willing to surrender my choices and activities to You. Cause me to desire the things You want me to do.

BE STILL

Thou wilt keep him in perfect peace, whose mind is stayed on thee: because he trusteth in thee.

ISAIAH 26:3 KJV

Longing for His children to know His peace, God sent prophets like Isaiah to stir up faith, repentance, and comfort in the hearts of the "chosen people."

God's message is just as applicable today as it was back then. By keeping our minds fixed on Him, we can have perfect, abiding peace even in the midst of a crazy world. The path to peace is not easy, but it is simple: Focus on God. As we meditate on His promises and His faithfulness, He gets bigger, while our problems get smaller.

God, when I focus on the world, my mind and heart feel anxious. Help me to keep my mind on You, so that I can have hope and peace.

WHY NOT ME?

God gave Paul the power to perform unusual miracles. When handkerchiefs or aprons that had merely touched his skin were placed on sick people, they were healed.

ACTS 19:11–12 NLT

When his fellow missionary, Trophimus, fell sick, Paul was given no miracle to help him. When Timothy complained of frequent stomach problems, Paul had no miracle-working handkerchief for Timothy's misery. Paul himself suffered from an incurable ailment (2 Corinthians 12:7), yet he was willing to leave it with God. We, too, may be clueless as to why God miraculously heals some and not others. Like Paul, we must trust God when there's no miracle. Can we be as resilient as Job, who said, "Though he slay me, yet will I trust in him" (Job 13:15 KJV)? We can—waiting for the day when health problems and bad accidents and death cease forever (Revelation 21:4).

When healing doesn't come, Lord Jesus, give me grace to trust You more. Still I choose hope. Amen.

CHRIST IS RISEN TODAY!

"He isn't here! He is risen from the dead!"

LUKE 24:6 NLT

The power God used to raise Christ from the dead is the same power we have available to us each day to live according to God's will here on earth. What happened on Easter gives us hope for today and for all eternity.

If you haven't accepted Jesus Christ as your personal Savior, take the time right now and start your new life in Christ.

Dear Jesus, thank You for dying on the cross for me and taking away all my sin. You are alive and well, and I praise You today for all You are and all You have done. Amen.

FENCES

"If you keep My commandments, you will abide in My love, just as I have kept My Father's commandments and abide in His love."

JOHN 15:10 NKJV

God's commandments are much like the pasture fence. Sin is on the other side. His laws exist to keep us in fellowship with Him and to keep us out of things that are harmful to us that can lead to bondage. We abide in the loving presence of our heavenly Father by staying within the boundaries He has set up for our own good. He has promised to care for us and to do the things needful for us. His love for us is unconditional, even when we jump the fence into sin. But by staying inside the boundaries, we enjoy intimacy with Him.

Father, help me to obey Your commandments that are given for my good. Thank You for Your love for me.

HE HAS CHOSEN YOU

Therefore, as God's chosen people, holy and dearly loved, clothe yourselves with compassion, kindness, humility, gentleness and patience.

COLOSSIANS 3:12 NIV

No matter how athletic, beautiful, popular, or smart you are, you've probably experienced a time when you were chosen last or overlooked entirely. Being left out is a big disappointment of life on earth.

The good news is that this disappointment isn't part of God's kingdom. Even when others forget about us, God doesn't. He has handpicked His beloved children now and forever. The truth is that Jesus died for *everyone*—every man, woman, and child who has ever and will ever live. The Father chooses us all. All we have to do is grab a glove and join the team.

Father, thanks for choosing me. I don't deserve it, but You call me Your beloved child. Help me to remember others who may feel overlooked or unloved. Let Your love for them shine through me. Amen.

PRAYING WITH CONFIDENCE

For we do not have a high priest who is unable to empathize with our weaknesses, but we have one who has been tempted in every way, just as we are—yet he did not sin. Let us then approach God's throne of grace with confidence, so that we may receive mercy and find grace to help us in our time of need.

HEBREWS 4:15–16 NIV

There is no one like a sister. A sister is someone who "gets you." But even a sister's love cannot compare to Christ's love. However you're struggling, help is available through Jesus. Our Savior walked on this earth for thirty-three years. He was fully God *and* fully man. He got dirt under His fingernails. He felt hunger. He knew weakness. He was tempted. He felt tired. He "gets it."

Go boldly before the throne of grace as a daughter of God. Pray in Jesus' name for an outpouring of His grace and mercy in your life.

Father, I ask You boldly in the name of Christ to help me. My hope is in You alone. Amen.

THE BREATH OF GOD

Every part of Scripture is God-breathed and useful one way or another—showing us truth, exposing our rebellion, correcting our mistakes, training us to live God's way.

2 TIMOTHY 3:16 MSG

Do you spend time in God's Word each day? Do you let the breath of God wash over you and comfort you? Are you allowing His Word to penetrate your heart and show you where you've been wrong? If not, you are missing out on one of the most important ways that God chooses to communicate with us today. Ask the Lord for the desire to spend more time in His Word. Don't feel you have the time? Consider purchasing the Bible on CD, and listen to God's Word as you drive to work or school.

Father, Your Word is so important to me. Please give me the desire to spend more time in the Bible each day. Amen.

FOCUS TIME

In the morning, LORD, you hear my voice;
in the morning I lay my requests before
you and wait expectantly.
PSALM 5:3 NIV

What is the first thing you do each morning? Many of us hit the ground running, armed with to-do lists a mile long. While it doesn't ensure perfection, setting aside a short time each morning to focus on the Father and the day ahead can help prepare us to live more intentionally. During this time we, like Jesus, gain clarity, so that we can invest our lives in the things that truly matter.

Father, help me to take time each morning to focus on You and the day ahead. Align my priorities so that the things I do will be the things You want me to do.

ABIDING PEACE

He himself is our peace.

EPHESIANS 2:14 NIV

Regardless of life's circumstances, hope and peace are available if Jesus is there. You do not have to succumb to getting buffeted and beaten by the storms of life. Seek refuge in the center of the storm. Run to the arms of Jesus, the Prince of Peace. Let Him wipe your tears and calm your fears. Like the eye of the hurricane, His presence brings peace and calmness. Move yourself closer. Desire to be in His presence. For He Himself is your peace. As you abide in His presence, peace will envelop you. The raging around you may not subside, but the churning of your heart will. You will find rest for your soul.

Dear Lord, thank You for being our peace in the midst of life's fiercest storms. Amen.

CONFIDENCE

For I know that my redeemer liveth, and that he shall stand at the latter day upon the earth: and though after my skin worms destroy this body, yet in my flesh shall I see God.

JOB 19:25–26 KJV

Although we experience various difficulties throughout life, we can still look forward to the blessed future we have. No matter what our struggles are, our Lord controls.

Job had no idea what the purpose of his trial was, but he faced his troubles with confidence, knowing that ultimately he would emerge victorious. Too many times we view our own situations with self-pity rather than considering God's strength and trusting that His plan is perfect. What peace God offers when we finally cast our cares on Him and with great conviction declare, "I know that my redeemer liveth!"

O great Redeemer, in You I have confidence even when I don't understand life's trials. Please help me to live victoriously.

THE PERFECT REFLECTION

"Give careful thought to your ways."
HAGGAI 1:7 NIV

As we give careful thought to our ways, we should first look back to where we have come from and reflect on God's work in our lives. We are on a journey. Sometimes the road is difficult; sometimes the road is easy. We must consider where we were when God found us and where we are now through His grace. Even more importantly, we must think about the ways our present actions, habits, and attitudes toward God reflect our lives as Christians. Only when we are able honestly to assess our lives in Christ can we call on His name to help perfect our reflection.

Dear Lord, help me to look honestly at the ways I live and make changes where necessary. Amen.

HIS HEALING ABUNDANCE

*"Behold, I will bring it health and healing;
I will heal them and reveal to them the
abundance of peace and truth."*

JEREMIAH 33:6 NKJV

If we confess our sins to God, He will bring relief to our souls. When we're distressed, we have Jesus, the Prince of Peace, to give us peace. When our emotions threaten to overwhelm us, we can implore Jehovah-Rapha—the God Who Heals—to calm our anxious hearts. When we're physically sick, we can cry out to Jesus, our Great Physician. Whether our problems affect us physically, spiritually, mentally, or emotionally, we can trust that God will come to us and bring us healing. And beyond our temporal lives, we can look forward with hope to our heavenly lives. There we will be healthy, whole, and alive—forever.

---

*Jehovah-Rapha, thank You for healing me.
Help me do my part to seek health and the
abundance of peace and truth You provide.*

ALWAYS THINKING OF YOU

What is man that You are mindful of him,
and the son of man that You visit him?

PSALM 8:4 NKJV

Have you ever wondered what God thinks about? *You* are always on His mind. In all you think and do, He considers you and makes intercession for you. He knows the thoughts and intents of your heart. He understands you like no other person can. He knows your strengths and weaknesses, your darkest fears and highest hopes. He's constantly aware of your feelings and how you interact with or without Him each day.

God is always with you, waiting for you to remember Him—to call on Him for help, for friendship, for anything you need.

Lord, help me to remember You as I go throughout my day. I want to include You in my life and always be thinking of You too. Amen.

I LIFT MY EYES

I lift up my eyes to the mountains—where does my help come from? My help comes from the Lord, *the Maker of heaven and earth.*

Psalm 121:1–2 NIV

Adulthood is a time when decisions can be the most crucial. Challenges, failures, doubts, and fears may cloud decisions and cripple us into inaction because the end result is unknown. Career paths, relationships, and financial decisions are only some of the areas that cause concern. In all of those things, and in all of life, we shouldn't keep our eyes fixed on the end result, and we shouldn't keep our heads down and simply plow through. Instead, we must lift our eyes to the Lord. If we fix our focus on Jesus, we will see that He is prepared to lead and guide us through all of life's challenges.

Lord, I lift up my eyes to You. Please help me and guide me down the path of life. Let me never become so focused on my own goals or so busy about my work that I forget to look to You, for You are my help. Amen.

LASTING TREASURE

*"Beware! Guard against every kind of greed.
Life is not measured by how much you own."*

LUKE 12:15 NLT

The Lord never meant for us to be satisfied with temporary treasures. Earthly possessions leave us empty because our hearts are fickle. Once we gain possession of one thing, our hearts yearn for something else. Lasting treasure can only be found in Jesus Christ. He brings contentment so that the treasure chests of our souls overflow in abundance. Hope is placed in the Lord rather than our net-worth statement. Joy is received by walking with the Lord, not by chasing some fleeting fancy. Love is showered upon us as we grab hold of real life—life that cannot be bought, but that can only be given through Jesus Christ.

Dear Lord, may I be content with what You have given me. May I not wish for more material treasures, but seek eternal wealth from You. Amen.

POUR OUT PRAYERS

Trust in Him at all times, you people; pour out your heart before Him; God is a refuge for us.

PSALM 62:8 NKJV

The psalmist tells us to trust the Lord at all times and to pour out our hearts to Him. There is nothing we think or feel that He does not already know. He longs for us to come to Him, spilling out our thoughts, needs, and desires. God invites us to an open-ended conversation. He made us for a relationship with Him. He never tires of listening to His children.

The Lord is our helper. He is our refuge. He knows the solutions to our problems and the wisdom we need for living each day.

Lord, remind me of Your invitation to pour out my problems to You. You are my refuge and my helper. Help me to trust You with every detail of my life.

REDEMPTION

Put your hope in the LORD, for with the LORD is unfailing love and with him is full redemption.

PSALM 130:7 NIV

When God permits a redemption, or "buying back," of lost years and relationships, we get a black-and-white snapshot of the colorful mural of God's redemption of us in Christ. When we one day stand in His presence, we'll understand more clearly the marvelous scope of God's redeeming love—in ways we cannot now begin to imagine. . . in broken relationships we thought could never be restored.

I praise You, Father, for Your awesome redemption. Thank You that I've yet to see the scope of it all. Amen.

OUR CONFIDENCE

Have no fear of sudden disaster or of the ruin that overtakes the wicked, for the LORD will be at your side and will keep your foot from being snared.

PROVERBS 3:25–26 NIV

Whether our loved ones are in harm's way daily or not, all of us live in a dangerous world. And while we should take physical precautions, our best preparation is spiritual.

When we spend time with God and learn about His love for us and our families, we begin to realize that He will give us His grace when we need it. He promises to never leave us, and the more we come to know His love, the more we will rest in that promise.

God, thank You that You promise Your peace to those who seek You. Help me to rest in Your love for my family and me.

YOUR GLORIOUS FUTURE

"No eye has seen, no ear has heard,
no human mind has conceived"—the things
God has prepared for those who love him.

1 CORINTHIANS 2:9 NIV

God's promise for our future is so magnificent we can't even comprehend it. He has great plans for each of us, but we often become paralyzed by fear. Why? Because the past seems more comfortable. Because the future is uncertain.

While God doesn't give us a map of what our future is like, He does promise that it will be more than we could ever ask or imagine. What steps of faith do you need to take today to accept God's glorious future for your life?

God, Your ways are not my ways and Your plans are too wonderful for me to even comprehend. Help me to never be satisfied with less than Your glorious plans for my life.

SMILE, SMILE, SMILE

A cheerful look brings joy to the heart.

PROVERBS 15:30 NLT

Days may not go just as planned. We are all human, and we can't always control our circumstances. What we can control, however, is our attitude. Remember each day that you are a representative of Jesus Christ. As a Christian and a woman, it is important to model a godly attitude at all times. Even a small look or smile can help show others the love of God. Just because we don't feel like having a good attitude doesn't mean we shouldn't try. God tells us to praise Him always—in good times and in bad. Let that praise show on your face today.

Lord, I know I can choose my attitude. Help me to show Your love to others by having a positive attitude each day. Let Your glory show on my face. Amen.

PRAYER

Jesus often withdrew to lonely places and prayed.

LUKE 5:16 NIV

Jesus is our perfect role model. If He withdrew often to pray, shouldn't we? Do we think we can continually give to others without getting replenished ourselves? Make prayer a priority. Recognize that the Lord must daily fill your cup so that you will have something to give. Set aside a specific time, a specific place. Start slow. Give Him five minutes every day. As you are faithful, your relationship with Him will grow. Over time, you will crave the time spent together as He fills your cup to overflowing. Follow Jesus' example and pray!

Dear Lord, help me set aside time to pray each day. Please fill my cup so that I can share with others what You have given me. Amen.

SWEATING THE SMALL STUFF

Blessed are all who fear the Lord, who walk in obedience to him. You will eat the fruit of your labor; blessings and prosperity will be yours.

PSALM 128:1–2 NIV

The Lord showers us with many blessings each day—family, friends, education, job, good health, and a beautiful earth. But despite the gifts He gives, it's easy to get bogged down in the little things that go wrong. We're all human, and we sometimes focus on all the negatives rather than the positives in life. Next time you're feeling that "woe is me" attitude, remember that you are a child of God. Spend some time counting all the wonderful blessings that come from the Lord rather than the headaches from this earth.

Father, thank You that I am Your child. Remind me each day to count the many blessings You shower upon me, rather than focusing on the negatives of this world. Amen.

SEASONS OF CHANGE

The Spirit of God, who raised Jesus from the dead, lives in you. And just as God raised Christ Jesus from the dead, he will give life to your mortal bodies by this same Spirit living within you.

ROMANS 8:11 NLT

Change can be exciting or fearsome. Changing a habit or moving beyond your comfort zone can leave you feeling out of control. The power of God that formed the world, brought the dry land above the waters of the sea, and raised Jesus from the dead is alive and active today. Imagine what it takes to overcome the natural laws of gravity—to put the earth and seas in place. Imagine the power to bring the dead to life again. That same power is available to work out the details of your life.

Lord, I want to grow and fulfill all You've destined me to be. Help me to accept change and depend on Your strength to make the changes I need in my life today. Amen.

SENSE OF BELONGING

"All that the Father gives Me will come to Me, and the one who comes to Me I will by no means cast out."

JOHN 6:37 NKJV

We belong to Christ. When the Father calls us to come to Jesus, we belong to Him. This is an irrevocable transaction. We are His, given to Him by the Father. He does not refuse to save us. He will not refuse to help us. No detail of our lives is unimportant to Him. No matter what happens, He will never let us go. Like the enduring love of a parent—but even more perfect—is the love of Christ for us. He has endured all the temptations and suffered all the pain that we will ever face. He has given His very life for us. We can live peacefully and securely knowing we belong to Him.

Lord Jesus, I confess I often forget that I belong to You and how much You love me. Help me to rest in Your everlasting love and care. Amen.

OUR ROCK AND SAVIOR

"The LORD lives! Praise be to my Rock! Exalted be my God, the Rock, my Savior!"

2 SAMUEL 22:47 NIV

Throughout the Psalms, we read that David not only worshipped and praised God, but he also complained to Him, was honest with God about what he was feeling, and even admitted to being angry at God. Perhaps the most amazing thing about David, though, was his constant devotion and reliance on his Creator. Even though David is the powerful king of Israel, he praises God in 2 Samuel 22:47, calling Him his Rock and Savior. David knew that God was alive, and he also knew that he needed Him more than anything else in the world.

It's the same for us today!

Dear Lord, You are my Rock and my Savior. You are alive, and I praise You as God above all else. Thank You for Your love and power. Amen.

HOLD HIS HAND

"For I am the Lord *your God who takes hold of your right hand and says to you, Do not fear; I will help you."*

Isaiah 41:13 NIV

God desires to help us. When we walk through life hand in hand with God, we can face anything. His love covers us. His presence is our guard. We can do all things through Christ because we are given His strength. Do you feel as though you're walking through life alone? Do not fear. Are you in need of love, protection, courage, and strength? Reach out your hand. Allow Jesus to take hold of it. Receive His love and protection. Bask in His courage and strength. Take hold of His hand!

Dear Lord, thank You that I do not have to fear. You will help me by taking my hand. Amen.

TRUTH

"You will know the truth,
and the truth will set you free."
JOHN 8:32 NLT

What lies do you believe about yourself? How might those lies be preventing you from experiencing God's plan for *your* life?

The next time you're tempted to believe a lie, write it down. Then find a scripture passage that speaks truth over the situation. Write that scripture verse across the lie. Commit the truth to memory. Over time God's Word will transform your thinking and you'll begin to believe the truth. Then something amazing will happen—you'll be set free.

Father, thank You for the truth Your Word speaks about my life. Open my eyes to the truth and help me to believe it. Amen.

NEVER LOST FOR LONG

For "whoever calls on the name of the LORD shall be saved."
ROMANS 10:13 NKJV

You call out to God, but maybe for a little while you don't hear anything. You may have to listen intently for a while, but eventually you are reassured by His voice.

When He calls your name, you know you are safe. You may have to take a few steps in the dark, but by moving toward Him you eventually see clearly. A light comes on in your heart, and you recognize where you are and what you need to do to get back on the path God has set before you.

Heavenly Father, help me to stay focused on You. Show me how to remove distractions from my life so I can stay close to You. Amen.

A VALUABLE DEPOSIT

He anointed us, set his seal of ownership on us, and put his Spirit in our hearts as a deposit, guaranteeing what is to come.

2 CORINTHIANS 1:21–22 NIV

When we commit our lives to Christ, He doesn't let us flail around in this mixed-up world without any help. We have the deposit of the Holy Spirit with us all the time, and He also gives us His Word and the help of other Christians to keep us strong in the Lord. So whenever you feel alone or overwhelmed with life, remember that God has anointed you, set His seal upon you, and deposited the Holy Spirit right inside your heart. That is the most valuable deposit of all!

Dear Lord, thank You for depositing Your Holy Spirit in my heart to lead and guide me. Help me to listen. Amen.

FEAR AND DREAD

"What I feared has come upon me;
what I dreaded has happened to me."

JOB 3:25 NIV

Do we have a secret fear or dread? God knew Job's secret fears, but still called him "blameless and upright" (Job 1:8 NIV). God doesn't withhold His love if we harbor unspoken dread. He doesn't love us any less because of secret anxieties. The Lord "is like a father to his children . . .he remembers we are only dust" (Psalm 103:13–14 NLT). God never condemned Job (and He'll never condemn us) for private fears. He encourages us, as He did Job, to trust Him. He alone retains control over all creation and all circumstances (Job 38–41).

Father, please stay beside me when what
I dread most comes to me. Amen.

LIGHT IN THE DARK

The light shines in the darkness,
and the darkness has not overcome it.

JOHN 1:5 NIV

Jesus said in John 12:46 (NIV), "I have come into the world as a light, so that no one who believes in me should stay in darkness." He also promised that He is always with us. Because we have Him, we have light. If we fail to perceive it, if we seem to be living in darkness, perhaps we have turned our backs to the light of His countenance. Maybe we are covering our eyes with the cares of this world. Clouds of sin may be darkening our lives, but He has not left us. He promises us that in following Him we will not walk in darkness but have the light of life.

Lord Jesus, show me my blind spots. Where am I covering my own eyes or walking away from You? Turn me back to You, the light of life.

JUMPING HURDLES

God's way is perfect.
All the LORD's promises prove true.
PSALM 18:30 NLT

Maybe there are times when you just don't think you can take one more disappointment or hurt. That's the perfect time to draw strength from God and His Word. Meditate on encouraging scriptures, or play a song that you know strengthens your heart and mind. Ask God to infuse you with His strength, and you'll find the power to take another step, and another—until you find yourself on the other side of that challenge you're facing today.

God, give me strength each day to face the obstacles I am to overcome. I am thankful that I don't have to face them alone. Amen.

MY FUTURE IS IN YOUR HANDS

The Lord says, "I will guide you along the best pathway for your life. I will advise you and watch over you."

Psalm 32:8 NLT

Are plans running wild in your head? Remember that the Lord is watching over you, and He is there to guide you. He wants you to seek Him out. Don't try to make your dreams happen all by yourself. Get on your knees and ask Him to direct your plans each morning. Don't be afraid to put your future in His hands!

Father, thank You for always being faithful to me. Continue to watch over me and direct my path. Amen.

LEARN CONTENTMENT

I am not saying this because I am in need,
for I have learned to be content
whatever the circumstances.
PHILIPPIANS 4:11 NIV

Contentment is learned and cultivated. It is an attitude of the heart. It has nothing to do with material possessions or life's circumstances. It has everything to do with being in the center of God's will and knowing it. Contentment means finding rest and peace in God's presence—nothing more, nothing less. It is trusting that God will meet all of your needs. May we learn to say confidently, *"The Lord is my shepherd, I shall not want."* That is the secret of contentment.

Dear Lord, teach me how to be content in You,
knowing that You will provide all that I need. Amen.

HE IS FAITHFUL

If we are unfaithful, he remains faithful,
for he cannot deny who he is.

2 TIMOTHY 2:13 NLT

Sometimes we treat our relationship with God the same as we do with other people. We promise Him we'll start spending more time with Him in prayer and Bible study. Soon the daily distractions of life get in the way, and we're back in our same routine, minus prayer and Bible study.

Even when we fail to live up to our expectations, our heavenly Father doesn't pick up His judge's gavel and condemn us for unfaithfulness. Instead, He remains a faithful supporter, encouraging us to keep trying to hold up our end of the bargain. Take comfort in His faithfulness, and let that encourage you toward a deeper relationship with Him.

Father, thank You for Your unending faithfulness.
Every day I fall short of Your standards, but You're
always there, encouraging me and lifting me up.
Please help me to be more faithful to You—
in the big things and in the little things. Amen.

HEAVENLY APPRECIATION

God is not unjust; he will not forget your work and the love you have shown him as you have helped his people and continue to help them.

HEBREWS 6:10 NIV

Sometimes it seems our hard work is ignored. When our work for Christ seems to go unnoticed by our church family, we can be assured that God sees our hard work and appreciates it. We may not receive the "church member of the month" award, but our love for our brothers and sisters in Christ and our work on their behalf is not overlooked by God. The author of Hebrews assures us that God is not unjust—our reward is in heaven.

Dear Lord, You are a God of love and justice. Even when I do not receive the notice of those around me, help me to serve You out of my love for You. Amen.

SPIRIT AND TRUTH

*"But the time is coming—indeed it's here now—
when true worshipers will worship the
Father in spirit and in truth."*

JOHN 4:23 NLT

God is everywhere all the time, and He doesn't just want to be worshipped at church. You can worship God on your way to work, during class, as you clean your house, and while paying your bills. Worship is about living your life in a way that is pleasing to the Lord and seeking Him first in all things. Paying your bills? Ask God how He wants you to spend your money. That is pleasing to Him, and that is worship. In the middle of class? Be respectful of your professors, and use the brain God gave you to complete your studies.

If you are living your everyday life to please God, that is worship!

---

*Father, help me to live my life in ways that
please You. Let my focus be on worshipping
You in everything I do. Amen.*

CHANGING OUR PERSPECTIVE

Turn my eyes away from worthless things;
preserve my life according to your word.

PSALM 119:37 NIV

The book of Psalms offers hundreds of verses that can easily become sentence prayers. "Turn my eyes from worthless things" whispered before heading out to shop, turning on the television, or picking up a magazine can turn those experiences into opportunities to see God's hand at work in our lives. He can change our perspective. He will show us what has value for us. He can even change our appetites, causing us to desire the very things He wants for us. When we pray this prayer, we are asking God to show us what He wants for us. He knows us and loves us more than we know and love ourselves. We can trust His love and goodness to provide for our needs.

Father, imprint this scripture in my mind today.
In moments of need, help me remember to pray
this prayer and to relinquish my desires to You.

GOD AS HE REALLY IS

The Lord *is compassionate and gracious, slow to anger, abounding in love. . . . He does not treat us as our sins deserve or repay us according to our iniquities.*

Psalm 103:8, 10 NIV

Our attitude toward God can influence the way we handle what He has given us. Some people perceive God as a harsh and angry judge, impatiently tapping His foot, saying, "When will you ever get it right?" People who see God this way can become paralyzed by an unhealthy fear of Him. However, the Bible paints a very different picture of God. Psalm 103 says He is gracious and compassionate, that He does not treat us as our sins deserve. What difference can it make in your life to know that you serve a loving God who is longing to be gracious to you?

Lord, thank You for Your compassion, Your grace, and Your mercy. Help me to see You as You really are.

LIVING A COMPLETE LIFE

It is a good thing to receive wealth from God and the good health to enjoy it.

ECCLESIASTES 5:19 NLT

God has promised to supply all your needs, but it takes action on your part. Seeking wisdom for your situation and asking God to direct you in the right decisions will help you find a well-balanced life that will produce success coupled with the health to enjoy it. It may be as simple as realizing a vacation is exactly what you need instead of working throughout the year and taking your vacation in cash to pay for new bedroom furniture.

Know when to press forward and when to stop, and enjoy the life God has given you for His good pleasure—and yours!

Lord, I ask for Your wisdom to help me balance my life so I can be complete in every area of my life. Amen.

FAITH AND ACTION

And I keep praying that this faith we hold in common keeps showing up in the good things we do, and that people recognize Christ in all of it.

PHILEMON 1:6 MSG

Our actions and reactions are a powerful gauge of how serious we are about our faith. When others wrong us, do we refuse to forgive and thus risk misrepresenting Christ, or do we freely offer forgiveness as an expression of our faith? God calls us to faith and forgiveness in Christ Jesus so that Christians and non-Christians alike will see our good deeds and praise God.

Dear Lord, please let me remember that people look to me for a glimpse of You. Let my actions always reflect my faith in You. Amen.

HOLDING THE LINE

When I said, "My foot is slipping," your unfailing love, Lord, supported me. When anxiety was great within me, your consolation brought me joy.

Psalm 94:18–19 NIV

Often we may feel that our feet are slipping in life. We lose our grip. Anxiety becomes a sleep robber, headache giver, and joy squelcher. Fear takes over our hearts. All we can think is, *Just get me out of here!* But we must remember who is anchoring our life. God's powerful grip secures us—even in the most difficult times. He comforts us with His loving presence that defies understanding. He provides wisdom to guide our steps through life's toughest challenges. We can rest assured that His support is steady, reliable, and motivated by His love for us.

Jesus, my rock and fortress, thank You that Your strength is made available to me. Steady me with the surety of Your love. Replace my anxiety with peace and joy, reflecting a life that's secured by the Almighty. Amen.

STANDING FIRM

I. . .didn't dodge their insults, faced them as they spit in my face. And the Master, God, stays right there and helps me, so I'm not disgraced. Therefore I set my face like flint, confident that I'll never regret this. My champion is right here. Let's take our stand together!

Isaiah 50:6–8 MSG

Isaiah reminds us that we are not alone in our battles—even when everyone is against us and we feel outnumbered and outmaneuvered. But remember, your champion, God, is right there, saying, "I am not leaving you! We are sticking this out together. You can put your chin up confidently, knowing that I, the Sustainer, am on your side. Let's take our stand together!"

Lord, boldly stand beside me. May the strength of Your arms gird me as I take a stand for You. Lift my chin today; give me confidence to face opposition, knowing You are right there with me. Amen.

SECURE IN TRUTH

Throw off your old sinful nature and your former way of life, which is corrupted by lust and deception. Instead, let the Spirit renew your thoughts and attitudes. Put on your new nature, created to be like God—truly righteous and holy.

EPHESIANS 4:22–24 NLT

In Christ, we have a new mind-set—fresh thinking. We know we are loved and treasured. The very God who spoke the universe into existence loved us enough to leave heaven and live in this imperfect world so He could save us from eternity in the hell we so deserved. Talk about significance! The delusions of this world fall away in light of who He is and what He has done for love of us. Our daily intake of His Word secures us in those truths. The lies of the evil one become ineffective.

Christ, rid me of my old way of thinking. Put the new mindset within me to see daily the lies I fall for. Help me to walk in rightness and holiness, reflecting You in all I am. Amen.

OBJECT OF FAITH

"And as Moses lifted up the serpent in the wilderness, even so must the Son of Man be lifted up, that whoever believes in Him should not perish but have eternal life."

JOHN 3:14–15 NKJV

When Nicodemus inquires of Jesus how a man receives eternal life, Jesus recalls this Old Testament image. Knowing He would be lifted up on a cross, the Lord Jesus points Nicodemus and us to faith in Him alone. We must repent of our sin and believe in the Son of God who died on the cross. Sin and its consequences are around us like serpents, but into the midst of our fallen world, God has sent Jesus to save us. He is the object of our faith. The crucified and resurrected Christ is the answer. He is the truth, the way, and the life.

Father, fix my gaze on Your Son lifted up for me.

NEVER FORGOTTEN

The Lord will keep you from all harm—he will watch over your life; the Lord will watch over your coming and going both now and forevermore.

Psalm 121:7–8 NIV

Our lives are like an ancient city contained within walls. In an ancient city, the gatekeeper's job was to make decisions about what went in and out of the city. God is the gatekeeper of our lives. He is always watching, always guarding, and ever vigilant in His care of us, even when we are least aware that He is doing so. Proverbs 2:8 (NKJV) says, "He guards the paths of justice, and preserves the way of His saints." By sending His Son to save us and His Spirit to dwell in us, He has assured us that we are never forgotten and never alone.

Forgive me, Father, for how often I forget about You. Help me remember that You are guarding and preserving me and that nothing comes into my life without Your permission.

CHOSEN

"I have chosen you and have not rejected you."

ISAIAH 41:9 NIV

The Lord doesn't dump us when we don't measure up. And He doesn't choose us one minute only to reject us a week later. We need not fear being deserted by our loving Father. He doesn't accept or reject us based on any arbitrary standards. He loves us with an everlasting love (Jeremiah 31:3). By His own mercy and design, "he hath made us accepted in the beloved" (Ephesians 1:6 KJV).

Father, thank You that I don't need to fear Your rejection of me. Amen.

PROMISES OF GOD

"For the LORD your God is living among you. He is a mighty savior. He will take delight in you with gladness. With his love, he will calm all your fears. He will rejoice over you with joyful songs."

ZEPHANIAH 3:17 NLT

Look at all the promises packed into this one verse of scripture! God is with you. He is your mighty Savior. He delights in you with gladness. He calms your fears with His love. He rejoices over you with joyful songs. Wow! What a bundle of hope is found here for the believer. Like a mother attuned to her newborn baby's cries, so is your heavenly Father's heart for you. He delights in being your Father. You are blessed to be a daughter of the King.

Father, thank You for loving me the way You do. You are all I need. Amen.

GET ABOVE IT ALL

Set your minds and keep them set on what is above (the higher things), not on the things that are on the earth.

COLOSSIANS 3:2 AMPC

Sometimes the most difficult challenges you face play out in your head—where a struggle to control the outcome and work out the details of life can consume you. Once removed—far away from the details—you can see things from a higher perspective. Close your eyes and push out the thoughts that try to grab you and keep you tied to the things of the world. Reach out to God and let your spirit soar. Give your concerns to Him and let Him work out the details. Rest in Him and He'll carry you above it all, every step of the way.

God, You are far above any detail of life that concerns me. Help me to trust You today for answers to those things that seem to bring me down. I purposefully set my heart and mind on You today.

THE LORD HIMSELF GOES BEFORE YOU

"The LORD himself goes before you and will be with you; he will never leave you nor forsake you. Do not be afraid; do not be discouraged."

DEUTERONOMY 31:8 NIV

Joshua 1:9 (NIV) tells us to "be strong and courageous. Do not be afraid; do not be discouraged, for the LORD your God will be with you wherever you go." Be encouraged! Even when it feels like it, you are truly never alone—and never without access to God's power. If you've trusted Christ as your Savior, the Spirit of God Himself is alive and well and working inside you at all times. What an astounding miracle! The Creator of the universe dwells within you and is available to encourage you and help you make right choices on a moment-by-moment basis.

Thank You, Lord, for the incredible gift of Your presence in each and every situation I face. Allow me to remember this and to call upon Your name as I go about each day.

SCRIPTURE INDEX

OLD TESTAMENT

Genesis
4:7 121
9:16 97
50:20 117

Exodus
14:14 24
15:20 88

Deuteronomy
11:18–20 10
31:8 187
33:25 38

Joshua
6:25 82

2 Samuel
22:47 162

Ezra
9:8 73

Nehemiah
1:4 86

Job
3:25 167
6:11 96
8:13 76
8:21 69
14:7 91
17:15 74
19:25–26 147
38:12–13 110

Psalms
1:2 46
5:3 . . . . 16, 145
8:4 150
9:1 67
10:14 113
18:30 169
22:11 56
27:1 . . . . 66, 105
32:8 . . . . 101, 170
33:18 71
35:22–24 108
37:1 104
37:4 131
37:23–24 59
42:5–6 41
42:8 107
42:11 25
46:1 72
62:5–6 5
62:8 153
71:5 15
94:18–19 179

103:8, 10 176
107:28–30 47
107:35 84
116:1 12
119:37 175
119:43 98
119:49 75
119:174–175 133
121:1–2 151
121:7 68
121:7–8 183
128:1–2 159
130:7 .... 62, 154
138:2 23
138:8 27
139:23–24 22
143:8 137
147:3 .... 51, 115

Proverbs

3:4 125
3:5–6 52
3:25–26 155
13:12 .... 39, 70
15:30 157
31:30 119

Ecclesiastes

3:1 32
3:11 102
5:19 177
7:14 112
8:5 42
9:4 78

Isaiah

26:3 138
29:13 127
40:31 57
41:9 184
41:13 163
43:19 100
50:6–8 180
54:5 132

Jeremiah

29:11 .... 14, 55
33:6 149

Lamentations

3:24 9
3:29 89

Ezekiel

36:26 87

Daniel

12:3 116

Hosea

2:16 17

Jonah

2:7 45

Micah

7:7 81
7:8 .... 40, 54

Zephaniah

3:17 185

Haggai

1:7 148

NEW TESTAMENT

Matthew

6:9–13 99
7:24–25 26

Mark

5:35 18
5:36 129
9:24 126

Luke

1:52 77
5:16 158
12:15 152
12:27–28 136
24:6 140

John

1:4–5 58
1:5 168
3:14–15 182
3:16 60
4:23 174
6:37 161
8:32 164
14:26 130
15:5 135
15:10 141
16:33 28

Acts

1:8 50
5:39–41 37
6:4 90
13:15 63
17:27 94
19:11–12 139

Romans

4:18 80
5:3–4 44
5:8 124
8:11 160
8:28 . . . . 43, 103
8:39 79
10:13 165
12:6–8 53
12:10 122
12:12 30
15:4 61
15:8 64

1 Corinthians
2:9 . . . 156
3:1–2 . . . 120
3:6 . . . 106
9:25 . . . 114

2 Corinthians
1:21–22 . . . 166

Galatians
5:1 . . . 123

Ephesians
1:4 . . . 85
1:18–19 . . . 11
1:19 . . . 93
2:10 . . . 19
2:14 . . . 146
3:20 . . . 7
4:22–24 . . . 181
5:16 . . . 20

Philippians
1:6 . . . 65
4:11 . . . 171

Colossians
1:13–14 . . . 29
1:17 . . . 111
3:2 . . . 186
3:12 . . . 142

1 Thessalonians
5:11 . . . 48
5:18 . . . 134

2 Thessalonians
2:16 . . . 83

1 Timothy
1:16 . . . 92
6:17 . . . 35

2 Timothy
2:13 . . . 172
3:16 . . . 144
4:7 . . . 118

Titus
1:2 . . . 31, 95

Philemon
1:6 . . . 178

Hebrews
4:15–16 . . . 143
6:10 . . . 173
10:23 . . . 34
11:1 . . . 21
12:2 . . . 33
13:20–21 . . . 128

1 Peter
3:15 . . . 8
3:15–16 . . . 36
4:8 . . . 109

2 Peter
1:5 . . . 49

Revelation
22:13 . . . 13